# Summary

Regardless of the outcome of the ongoing debate about the proposed Yucca Mountain geologic waste repository in Nevada, the storage of spent nuclear fuel (SNF)—also referred to as "high-level nuclear waste"—will continue to be needed and the issue will continue to be debated. The need for SNF storage, even after the first repository is opened, will continue for a few reasons.

- The Obama Administration terminated work on the only planned permanent geologic repository at Yucca Mountain, which was intended to provide a destination for most of the stored SNF. Also, the Yucca Mountain project was not funded by Congress in FY2011 and FY2012, and not included in the Administration's budget request for FY2013.

- Even if the planned repository had been completed, the quantity of SNF and other high-level waste in storage awaiting final disposal now exceeds the legal limit for the first repository under the Nuclear Waste Policy Act (NWPA).

- The expected rate of shipment of SNF to the repository would require decades to remove existing SNF from interim storage. Accordingly, the U.S. Nuclear Regulatory Commission (NRC) and reactor operators are considering extended SNF storage lasting for more than 100 years.

The debate about SNF typically involves where and how it is stored, as well as what strategies and institutions should govern SNF storage. The earthquake and tsunami in Japan, and resulting damage to the Fukushima Dai-ichi nuclear power plant, caused some in Congress and NRC to consider the adequacy of protective measures at U.S. reactors. The NRC Near-Term Task Force on the disaster concluded it has "not identified any issues that undermine our confidence in the continued safety and emergency planning of U.S. plants." Nonetheless, NRC has accepted a number of staff recommendations on near-term safety enhancement, including requirements affecting spent fuel storage and prevention and coping with station blackout. NRC is not requiring accelerated transfer of SNF from wet pools to dry casks, but the SNF storage data from the last several years indicate that accelerated transfer has already been occurring.

As of December 2011, more than 67,000 metric tons of SNF, in more than 174,000 assemblies, is stored at 77 sites (including 4 Department of Energy (DOE) facilities) in the United States located in 35 states (see **Table 1** and **Figure 5**), and increases at a rate of roughly 2,000 metric tons per year. Approximately 80% of commercial SNF is stored east of the Mississippi River. At 9 commercial SNF storage sites there are no operating nuclear reactors (so-called "stranded" SNF), and at the 4 DOE sites reactor operations largely ceased in the 1980s, but DOE-owned and some commercial SNF continues to be stored at DOE facilities. In the United States, SNF is stored largely at nuclear reactor sites where it was generated. Of the 104 operating nuclear reactors in the United States, all necessarily have wet storage pools for storing SNF (wet pools are required to allow for a safe "cooling off" period of 1 to 5 years after discharge of SNF from a reactor). Wet storage pools are used for storage of approximately 73% (49,338 out of 67,450 metric tons of uranium, or MTU) of the current commercial SNF inventory, whereas the remaining 27% (18,112 MTU) of commercial SNF is stored in dry casks on concrete pads or in vaults. As wet storage pools become filled to capacity using "dense packing" storage methods, dry storage is increasingly being used, although there are 27 sites with 36 wet storage pools with no current dry cask storage capabilities.

This report focuses on the current situation with spent nuclear fuel storage in the United States. It does not address all of the issues associated with permanent disposal of SNF, but rather focuses on the SNF storage situation, primarily at current and former reactor facilities for the potentially foreseeable future.

# Contents

# Figures

# Tables

# Appendixes

# Contacts

# Introduction

Recent events have renewed long-standing congressional interest in safe management of spent nuclear fuel (SNF) and other high-level nuclear waste.[1] These issues have been examined and debated for decades, sometimes renewed by world events like the 9/11 terrorist attacks. The incident at the Fukushima Dai-ichi nuclear reactor complex in Japan, combined with the termination of the Yucca Mountain geologic repository project,[2] have contributed to the increased interest.

This report focuses on the current situation with spent nuclear fuel storage in the United States. It does not address all of the issues associated with permanent disposal of SNF, but rather focuses on the SNF storage situation, primarily at current and former reactor facilities and former reactor sites for the potentially foreseeable future (i.e., a total of 300 years).[3]

Although no nation has yet established a permanent disposal repository for SNF and other forms of high-level radioactive waste (HLW), there is broad consensus that a geological repository is the preferred method for these wastes.[4] In the United States, the disposal repository location has been debated for decades. The proposed repository in Nevada at Yucca Mountain was terminated in 2009, although the project continues to be debated and litigated. Whether the current situation with the Yucca Mountain project is merely a temporary hiatus or becomes a permanent shutdown, extended storage for longer than previously anticipated is virtually assured. There is also no clear consensus on interim storage of SNF. The SNF storage issues most widely debated include

- What strategies should be employed for SNF storage, pending disposal;

- Where should SNF be stored on an interim basis; and

- What SNF management structure should be used?

---

[1] "Spent Nuclear Fuel" (SNF) is sometimes referred to as "used" nuclear fuel. This difference in terminology often reflects a significant policy debate about whether SNF is a waste destined for disposal, or a resource. This report uses the term SNF to be consistent with other independent agency documentation. The broader term, "nuclear waste," which is sometimes used to refer to SNF, is generally not used here to avoid imprecision and confusion with other waste forms (e.g., low-level or transuranic waste and naturally occurring radioactive materials). Although they are quite different technically, spent nuclear fuel and liquid raffinate waste from reprocessing are both defined legally under the Nuclear Waste Policy Act (NWPA) as "high-level waste." See 42 U.S.C. 10101(2)(12) and 10 C.F.R. 60.2, 10 C.F.R. 63.2, and 40 C.F.R. 197.2.

[2] House Energy and Commerce Committee; Environment Subcommittee Hearing, "DOE's Role in Managing Civilian Radioactive Waste," June 1, 2011, http://energycommerce house.gov/news/PRArticle.aspx?NewsID=8710; and House Energy and Commerce Subcommittee on Environment and the Economy, "Bipartisan Concern Over Administration's Haste to Terminate Permanent Nuclear Repository," press release, June 15, 2011.

[3] See CRS Report R40202, *Nuclear Waste Disposal: Alternatives to Yucca Mountain*, by Mark Holt; and CRS Report RL33461, *Civilian Nuclear Waste Disposal*, by Mark Holt, for discussion of related issues.

[4] See, e.g., National Research Council, Board on Radioactive Waste Management, *Rethinking High-Level Radioactive Waste Disposal: A Position Statement of the Board on Radioactive Waste Management* (1990), p. 2. National Academies/National Research Council/Board on Radioactive Waste Management, *Disposition of High-Level Waste and Spent Nuclear Fuel: The Continuing Societal and Technical Challenges*, National Academy Press, Washington, DC, 2001; Massachusetts Institute of Technology, *The Future of the Nuclear Fuel Cycle: An Interdisciplinary MIT Study*, MIT, Cambridge, MA, 2011; and Matthew Bunn, et al., *Interim Storage of Spent Nuclear Fuel: A Safe, Flexible, and Cost-Effective Near Term Approach to Spent Nuclear Fuel Management*, Harvard Press, Cambridge, MA, Harvard University Project on Managing the Atom and University of Tokyo Project on Nuclear Energy, 2001, http://belfercenter ksg harvard.edu/files/spentfuel.pdf.

---

A focus of this renewed broader debate is the recently completed report by the Blue Ribbon Commission on America's Nuclear Future (BRC), which released its final report on January 29, 2012.[5] This final report modified a July 2011 draft, which followed nearly more than a year of effort, including extensive public testimony and several subcommittee reports after the Commission was chartered by the Secretary of Energy in early 2010.[6]

Some, including the U.S. Nuclear Regulatory Commission (NRC), view the current situation as providing adequate safety. Others, including the National Academy of Sciences, have observed that safety may be improved by wider use of dry storage methods. Some analysts, including the BRC, have considered issues beyond safety—including cost and impact on investments—and urge construction of an interim centralized storage at a "volunteer" location after sufficient cooling has occurred.[7]

Some have recommended a more limited approach to consolidation of interim SNF storage using a smaller number of existing operational reactor sites, away from the original generating reactor, for SNF located where there is no operating reactor generating additional SNF or if repository delays result in greater stranded SNF and higher financial liabilities.[8] The two primary technologies being employed in the United States are wet pool storage and dry cask storage (see "How Is Spent Fuel Stored Now?").

| **Spent Nuclear Fuel (SNF) In Brief** |
| --- |
| • Commercial SNF is composed of metal assemblies about 12'-15' long (**Figure 1**). |
| • SNF contains uranium and elements created in nuclear reaction. |
| • SNF assemblies are removed from reactors after being used to produce power. |
| • Existing reactors generate about 2,000 metric tons per year. |
| • More than 67,000 metric tons of commercial SNF is currently being stored. |
| • Most SNF is stored at 77 sites in 35 states (see **Figure 5**). |
| • Some SNF is stored at closed reactors. |
| • Some SNF is stored at Department of Energy (DOE) facilities. |
| • Only 4% of the SNF in the United States is DOE-owned. |
| • SNF is stored in wet pools and dry casks. |
| • SNF storage at reactors was intended to be temporary, pending disposal. |
| • No nation operates a disposal site for SNF. |
| • Proposed U.S. disposal site for SNF at Yucca Mountain in Nevada was terminated in 2009. |
| • SNF storage is expected to be needed for more than 100 years. |

---

[5] Blue Ribbon Commission on America's Nuclear Future, *Report to the Secretary of Energy*, January 2012, http://brc.gov/sites/default/files/documents/brc_finalreport_jan2012.pdf.

[6] Blue Ribbon Commission on America's Nuclear Future, U.S. Department of Energy, Advisory Committee Charter, filed with Congress March 1, 2010. See http://brc.gov/index.php?q=page/charter.

[7] Kraft, Steven P., "Used Nuclear Fuel Integrated Management," Nuclear Energy Institute, Presentation to National Association of Regulatory Utility Commissioners (NARUC), February 13, 2010; Redmond, Everett, "Nuclear Energy Institute Comments on the Disposal Subcommittee Draft Report to the Blue Ribbon Commission on America's Nuclear Future," July 1, 2011 (see http://brc.gov/sites/default/files/comments/attachments/comments_of_nuclear_energy_institute_-_july_1_2011.pdf), and Kraft, Steven P., "Used Nuclear Fuel Integrated Management," Nuclear Energy Institute, Presentation to National Association of Regulatory Utility Commissioners (NARUC), February 13, 2010.

[8] Cochran, Thomas B. (Natural Resources Defense Council, Inc.), "Statement on the Fukushima Nuclear Disaster and its Implications for U.S. Nuclear Power Reactors," Joint Hearings of the Subcommittee on Clean Air and Nuclear Safety and the Committee on Environment and Public Works, U.S. Senate, April 12, 2011, and American Physical Society Nuclear Energy Study Group, *Consolidated Interim Storage of Commercial Spent Nuclear Fuel: A Technical and Programmatic Assessment*, February 2007.

---

Senator Dianne Feinstein, chair of the Senate Subcommittee on Energy and Water Development Appropriations, with jurisdiction over NRC and the U.S. Department of Energy (DOE), stated at a hearing in March 2011:

> Most significantly, I believe we must rethink how we manage spent fuel. Spent fuel must remain in pools for at least five to seven years, at which time it can be moved to safer dry cask storage. However, these pools often become de facto long-term storage, with fuel assemblies "re-racked" thus increasing the heat load of the pools. In California, for instance, fuel removed from reactors in 1984 is still cooling in wet spent fuel pools.... Reports out of Japan indicate there were no problems with the dry casks at Dai-ichi. To me, that suggests we should at least consider a policy that would encourage quicker movement of spent fuel to dry cask storage.[9]

Senator Feinstein followed up this hearing statement with a formal letter to the NRC chairman asking NRC "to seriously consider regulatory policies that would encourage the movement of nuclear fuel, once sufficiently cool, out of spent fuel pools and into dry cask storage systems."[10] Citing the 2006 study by the National Academy of Sciences (NAS) National Research Council (*Safety and Security of Commercial Spent Nuclear Fuel Storage*), Senator Feinstein specifically asked the "NRC to initiate a rulemaking process to immediately require a more rapid shift of spent fuel to dry casks."[11] Senator Feinstein indicated her concern about spent fuel management in evaluating proposals for funding small modular reactors.[12] NRC subsequently considered SNF storage needs a part of its Near-Term Task Force on the Fukushima Dai-ichi incident.

A House Appropriations Subcommittee report recently expressed concern about current spent fuel storage, indicating that "[c]onsolidation of this material in a single site that provides enhanced safety and security will improve public comfort with nuclear power, reduce potential safety and security risk, and fulfill the federal government's obligation under the Nuclear Waste Policy Act of 1982 to assume responsibility of spent fuel."[13] Although consolidated interim storage of SNF has received widespread support as a general concept for many years, proposals for SNF storage at specific locations have been vigorously opposed.[14]

The issue of SNF storage is inextricably linked to related longer-term issues like nuclear power plant operations and construction, SNF reprocessing, and establishment of a permanent repository. This report is focused on SNF storage, and does not provide a detailed examination of these related issues.[15]

---

[9] Chairman Dianne Feinstein, Opening Statement, Hearing of the Senate Committee on Appropriations Subcommittee on Energy and Water Development, "U.S. Nuclear Power Safety in Light of Japan Disaster," March 30, 2011.

[10] Senator Dianne Feinstein, Letter to Gregory Jaczko, Chairman of U.S. Nuclear Regulatory Commission, April 8, 2011.

[11] Ibid.

[12] Senator Dianne Feinstein, Safety and Economics of Light Small Water Modular Reactors, Statement at Hearing on Light Small Water Modular Reactors, Senate Energy and Water Development Appropriations Subcommittee, June 14, 2011.

[13] U.S. House Energy and Water Development Appropriations Subcommittee, *112th Congress Report; 1st Session; Energy and Water Development Appropriations Bill Committee Report*, 2012 (June 2011). Also see Committee on Science, Space, and Technology, Majority Staff Report; "Yucca Mountain: The Administration's Impact on U.S. Nuclear Waste Management Policy," June 2011.

[14] See generally, Walker, J. Samuel (NRC Historian), *The Road To Yucca Mountain: The Development of Radioactive Waste Policy in the United States*, University of California Press, 2009.

[15] See CRS Report R40202, *Nuclear Waste Disposal: Alternatives to Yucca Mountain*, by Mark Holt, and CRS Report (continued...)

Worldwide, there are 436 operational nuclear power reactors in 32 countries and 122 permanently shut-down nuclear power reactors, including several in countries where SNF continues to be stored after the reactor fleet has been shut down.[16] No country, including the United States, has yet established an operating permanent disposal site for SNF or other forms of high-level nuclear waste. All nations rely—to varying degrees—on long-term SNF storage.[17] Although the United States has not fully addressed its nuclear waste issues, DOE has, since 1999, operated a permanent geological repository for plutonium-contaminated transuranic (i.e., mainly plutonium-contaminated)[18] waste from nuclear weapons operations[19] in New Mexico. Known as the Waste Isolation Pilot Plant (WIPP), this waste disposal repository was constructed and began operations following decades of detailed technical and institutional planning, active state and community involvement,[20] and compliance work to meet various federal and state environmental review and permitting requirements.[21] The WIPP site is explicitly prohibited by law from receiving SNF or high-level waste, but is widely regarded as a model for other waste facility—both disposal and storage—siting efforts. A recent survey of spent fuel storage in the 10 countries with significant nuclear operations found that all countries store substantial amounts of SNF in pools or dry cask facilities,[22] regardless of their policy on reprocessing.[23]

---

(...continued)

RL34234, *Managing the Nuclear Fuel Cycle: Policy Implications of Expanding Global Access to Nuclear Power*, coordinated by Mary Beth Nikitin.

[16] International Atomic Energy Agency, Nuclear Power Reactors in the World, 2010 Edition (Reference Data Series No. 2), IAEA, Vienna, Austria. See http://www-pub.iaea.org/MTCD/Publications/PDF/iaea-rds-2-30_web.pdf.

[17] Finland (with four nuclear reactors) is the only country where a commercial nuclear waste repository site has been selected with local government involvement and support, and characterization work has begun for a permanent high-level radioactive repository. Sweden has operated an interim central SNF pool storage facility since 1985 at Oskarshamn, and plans to develop a permanent geologic repository about 200 miles north at the Forsmark nuclear power plant near Östhammar, which has a right to veto the permit. France has a strongly supported nuclear power program, but has not yet selected a disposal site for the high-level waste and SNF (approximately 13,500 MT of SNF (as of 2007) and 2,229 cubic meters of vitrified high-level waste (as of 2007) were stored in France).

[18] "Transuranic" waste is defined as alpha-emitting radioactive waste contaminated with radionuclides heavier than uranium (atomic weight 93) at a concentration greater than 100 nCi/g (3.7 MBq/kg). The Waste Isolation Pilot Plant Land Withdrawal Act as amended by P.L. 104-201 (H.R. 3230, 104th Congress)."

[19] de Saillan, Charles, "Disposal of Spent Nuclear Fuel in the United States and Europe: A Persistent Environmental Problem," *Harvard Environmental Law Review* 34, 461 (2010).

[20] See generally McCutcheon, Chuck, *Nuclear Reactions, The Politics of Opening a Radioactive Waste Disposal Site*, University of New Mexico Press, 2002, ISBN-10: 0826322093.

[21] The opening and operation of WIPP is given by some as evidence that the "nuclear waste problem" can be solved. While recognizing the successful siting and permitting of WIPP, others note inherent uncertainty about long-term performance. Also, some have suggested that the WIPP site be used later for disposal of high-level waste and spent nuclear fuel, in addition to disposal of transuranic wastes for which it is currently dedicated. Such a change of mission at WIPP would require, at a minimum, amending Section 12 of the WIPP Land Withdrawal Act, which provides a "ban on high-level radioactive waste and spent nuclear fuel." P.L. 102-579, 106 Stat. 4777.

[22] An SNF storage "facility" is generally associated with a reactor (see **Figure 2** and **Figure 3**), except in the case of the Morris, IL, facility, which was initially built not as a power reactor, but as part of an SNF reprocessing facility that never operated. In many cases there are more than one nuclear power reactor and SNF storage "facility" at a "site," which is a geographically contiguous area (see "Where Is Spent Nuclear Fuel Located Now in the United States?"). Because dry cask storage areas are typically independent of a reactor facility at a site, dry cask storage is generally quantified according to number of sites, not facilities.

[23] Feiveson, Harold, Zia Mian, M.V. Ramana and Frank von Hippel, International Panel on Fissile Materials, "Spent Fuel from Nuclear Power Reactors: An Overview of a New Study by the International Panel on Fissile Materials," September 2011. The study summarizes SNF management in the United States, Canada, France, Germany, Finland, Japan, South Korea, Russia, Sweden, and the United Kingdom. France provides the greatest support for reprocessing its SNF, but is listed as having the third highest amount of SNF (13,500 MT in 2007), behind the U.S. and Canada.

---

Although much of the congressional attention has focused on the issues of the permanent geological repository proposed for Yucca Mountain in Nevada, there are a number of reasons to also consider SNF storage issues.

First, under any scenario for waste acceptance into a permanent repository or an interim consolidated storage site, long-term storage of SNF will be required for a considerable time. Notwithstanding the mandate in the Nuclear Waste Policy Act (NWPA) and various contracts that DOE begin accepting SNF for disposal in 1998, no disposal repository has been completed or licensed. The 2009 termination of the Yucca Mountain disposal project continues the ongoing delay in opening a permanent geologic repository.[24] Hence, the disposal delay prolongs storage needs.

Even if a disposal repository were to begin operation quickly, the time required to ship SNF would require an extended period of storage. In its most recent estimate, prior to termination of the Yucca Mountain repository program, DOE projected that, if waste acceptance were to begin in 2020, there would be a need for commercial interim storage until at least 2056, given this projected shipment rate and the continued generation of new SNF.[25]

Also, current law—the NWPA—sets a limit on how much waste can be put in the first repository, and the U.S. inventory of SNF and other high-level waste requiring disposal has already exceeded this limit. The NWPA "prohibit[s] the emplacement in the first repository of a quantity of spent fuel containing in excess of 70,000 metric tons of uranium (MTU)[26] or a quantity of solidified high-level radioactive waste resulting from the reprocessing of such a quantity of spent fuel until such time as a second repository is in operation."[27] Of this 70,000 MTU limit set by Congress on the first repository in the NWPA, approximately 90% (63,000 MTU) of the capacity is allocated to commercial spent nuclear fuel and high-level radioactive waste from reprocessing.[28] The remaining 10% capacity would be used for about 2,455 MTU of DOE spent nuclear fuel (including naval spent nuclear fuel) and the equivalent of 4,667 MTU of DOE high-level radioactive waste.[29] Hence, the current quantity of SNF (i.e., 67,450 MTU of civilian SNF and 2,458 MTU of DOE-owned SNF) and high-level waste being stored would fill the proposed Yucca Mountain repository beyond the limit imposed by Congress in the NWPA, necessitating a need to build a second repository or change the legal limit. DOE has evaluated the capacity of the proposed Yucca Mountain repository and concluded that Yucca Mountain could hold more than

---

[24] See "Hazards and Potential Risks Associated with SNF Storage" below.

[25] Christopher A. Kouts, Principal Deputy Director, Office of Civilian Radioactive Waste Management, U.S. Department of Energy, "Yucca Mountain Program Status Update," July 22, 2008, p. 18.

[26] Metric tons of uranium (MTU) is a common unit of measurement for SNF, which allows for consistent measurement/estimation of fuel burnup. In some cases SNF is measured by metric tons of heavy metal or initial heavy metal (to distinguish the uranium fuel from the metal cladding), which have significant differences for evaluating reactor operations, but the distinction reflects a relatively minor difference for measurement purposes in this overview of SNF inventory.

[27] 42 U.S.C. §10134.(d).

[28] Most reprocessing in the United States was performed for separation of nuclear materials for nuclear weapons and other defense purposes. A relatively small amount of high-level radioactive waste was generated at, and remains stored at, the West Valley site in New York, after being vitrified in the 1990s. Most of the material reprocessed at the West Valley site was civilian SNF.

[29] U.S. Department of Energy Office of Civilian Radioactive Waste Management, Final Supplemental Environmental Impact Statement for a Geologic Repository for the Disposal of Spent Nuclear Fuel and High-Level Radioactive Waste at Yucca Mountain, Nye County, Nevada Summary, DOE/EIS-0250F-S1, June 2008.

---

the legal limit of 70,000 MTU and "has the physical capability to allow disposal of a much larger inventory."[30]

If waste were accepted at a consolidated nuclear waste storage site, rather than a disposal repository, the need for interim storage technologies could continue for a longer period. Hence, the issues related to safe long-term SNF storage—regardless of the current debate about a permanent geologic repository—warrant consideration. A recent study by the Massachusetts Institute of Technology (MIT) concluded that "planning for the long term interim storage of spent nuclear fuel—for about a century—should be part of fuel cycle design."[31] The issues and options associated with current national policies are discussed below.

The recent change in the Yucca Mountain repository program is not the first time that concern about the path forward of a permanent geologic repository has caused increased attention to long-term, possibly consolidated, storage of SNF. After the failure of the salt dome waste repository program near Lyons, KS, the Atomic Energy Commission[32] proposed in 1972 a program for long-term (100-year) retrievable surface storage.[33] In 1987, the same amendments to the Nuclear Waste Policy Act (NWPA) that identified the Yucca Mountain site also established the Monitored Retrievable Storage Commission (ended in 1989) and a position of the "Nuclear Waste Negotiator," which was eliminated in 1995 after several years of unsuccessful attempts to find a voluntary host community for a repository or monitored retrievable storage facility for nuclear waste.[34] During the 1990s, Congress tried, unsuccessfully, to enact legislation to help establish a temporary consolidated storage site for commercial spent nuclear fuel near the Yucca Mountain site. A number of analysts[35] have found that interim on-site storage or SDNF using dry casks is a viable option, and some have recommended that interim storage of spent fuel be implemented deliberately for a period of at least 100 years.[36]

Second, SNF stored outside of a reactor comprises a source of radioactivity requiring durable protection. Although radioactive decay reduces the amount of radioactivity in SNF, dropping sharply soon after discharge from a reactor, SNF provides a significant and long-term radioactivity source term for risk analyses. While the nuclear fuel in an operating reactor typically contains a larger amount of radioactivity, in terms of curie content, than stored SNF, much of this curie content is composed of relatively short-lived fission products, and includes more volatile constituents, compared to SNF. Although there have been some releases of radioactivity from stored SNF (see "Hazards and Potential Risks Associated with SNF Storage" below), there is no evidence of any consequent significant public exposures or health impacts. Nonetheless,

---

[30] DOE, Office of Civilian Radioactive Waste Management, "The Report to the President and the Congress by the Secretary of Energy on the Need for a Second Repository," DOE/RW-0595; December 2008.

[31] Massachusetts Institute of Technology, *The Future of the Nuclear Fuel Cycle: An Interdisciplinary MIT Study*, MIT, Cambridge, MA, 2011, at page xi.

[32] The Atomic Energy Commission (AEC) was a predecessor to the U.S. Department of Energy (DOE). The Energy Research and Development Administration succeeded the AEC in 1975 and was replaced by DOE in 1978.

[33] Walker, J. Samuel (NRC Historian), *The Road to Yucca Mountain: The Development of Radioactive Waste Policy in the United States*, University of California Press, 2009; and Atomic Energy Commission Press Release, Frank K. Pittman, "Management of Commercial High-Level Nuclear Radioactive Waste," July 25, 1972, AEC Press release.

[34] 42 U.S.C. 10242.

[35] See Allison Macfarlane, "Interim Storage of Spent Fuel in the United States," *Annual Review of Energy and the Environment*, vol. 26, 2001.

[36] Arjun Makhijani and Scott Saleska, *High-Level Dollars, Low-Level Sense*, Institute for Energy and Environmental Research, Apex Publishers, Takoma Park, MD 1991.

---

significant concerns have been raised about the potential for releases from stored SNF.[37] These concerns have been heightened in the wake of the incident at the Fukushima Dai-ichi reactors in Japan, about which there have been conflicting accounts and some uncertainty regarding the condition of the stored SNF.

Extended storage has also raised concerns about long-term site safety. For example, in the wake of general concern about the risks from extreme weather and sea level rise from climate change, as well as specific concerns about SNF stored near flood-prone rivers (e.g., along the Missouri River), some have expressed urgency about the need to relocate SNF storage.[38] NRC, however, found that sea level rise was not a credible threat to existing and planned on-site nuclear waste storage for the next several decades: "Based on the models discussed in the [National Academy of Sciences/National Research Council study], none of the U.S. [Nuclear Power Plants] (operational or decommissioned) will be under water or threatened by water levels by 2050."[39]

Third, the federal government faces a significant and growing liability to pay claims resulting from its failure to begin accepting waste from commercial utilities under the 1987 NWPA.[40] The U.S. government[41] has paid approximately $1 billion[42] to pay a series of claims by utilities that DOE had, at least partially, breached its contracts to accept SNF.[43] The federal government has been paying claims for commercial utility costs for SNF storage since 2000.[44] These claims arise from the 76 standard contracts DOE signed in 1983, largely with commercial utilities, of which 74 have filed claims against DOE for damages arising from failure to accept the SNF by 1998.[45]

---

[37] Several states, including New York and Connecticut, have challenged NRC's "Waste Confidence" rule, which concluded that SNF "can be stored safely and without significant environmental impacts ..." (See United States Court of Appeals for the District of Columbia Circuit, *State of New York, et al., Petitioners, Nos. 11-1045, 11-1051, -against-11-1056, 11-1057 Nuclear Regulatory Commission and United States of America, Respondents*); and Alvarez, Robert, *Spent Nuclear Fuel Pools in the U.S.: Reducing the Deadly Risks of Stor*age, Institute for Policy Studies, May 2011; Zhang, Hui. *Radiological Terrorism: Sabotage of Spent Fuel Pools*, INESAP: International Network of Engineers and Scientists Against Proliferation no. 22 (December 2003): 75-78.

[38] A. G. Sulzberger and Matthew L. Wald, "Flooding Brings Worries Over Two Nuclear Plants," *New York Times*, June 20, 2011.

[39] U.S. Nuclear Regulatory Commission, "Consideration of Environmental Impacts of Temporary Storage of Spent Fuel After Cessation of Reactor Operations; Waste Confidence Decision Update; Final Rule," 75 *Federal Register* 81032, December 23, 2010; and National Academies/National Research Council, Committee on Climate Change and U.S. Transportation, *Potential Impact of Climate Change on U.S. Transportation: Special Report 290*, 2008.

[40] For more information on this liability issue, see CRS Report R40996, *Contract Liability Arising from the Nuclear Waste Policy Act (NWPA) of 1982*, by Todd Garvey.

[41] The claims have been paid from the "Judgment Fund," which is a permanent, indefinite appropriation for the payment of judgments against the United States managed by the U.S. Department of Justice (see 31 U.S.C. §1304), not from appropriations to DOE through the Energy and Water Development Subcommittees. The U.S. government cannot use the Nuclear Waste Fund to pay for any of the damages that the utilities incur as a result of DOE's delay, because on-site storage is not one of the uses of the NWF authorized by the NWPA (see Alabama Power Co. v. United States Department of Energy, 307 F.3d 1300 (11th Cir. 2002)).

[42] U.S. Government Accountability Office, GAO-11-731T, *Nuclear Waste, Disposal Challenges and Lessons Learned from Yucca Mountain*, June 1, 2011, http://www.gao.gov/new.items/d11731t.pdf.

[43] The utilities' damages claims largely consist of the costs incurred to store SNF. The costs include capital costs to construct dry storage facilities or additional wet storage racks, costs to purchase and load casks and canisters, and costs of utility personnel necessary to design, license, and maintain these storage facilities.

[44] Court of Appeals for the Federal Circuit, in *Maine Yankee Atomic Power Co. v. United States*, 225 F.3d 1336, 1343 (Fed. Cir. 2000). and *Pac. Gas & Elec. Co. v. United States*, 536 F. 3d 1282, 1284, 1287 (Fed. Cir. 2008.)

[45] Michael F. Hertz, U.S. Department of Justice, *Statement Before the Blue Ribbon Commission on America's Nuclear Future*, February 2, 2011.

---

The future estimated costs for storage of commercial SNF are approximately $500 million per year.[46]

Fourth, some have argued that the uncertainty and concerns about nuclear waste management have contributed to the lack of investment in new nuclear power plants, resulting in a failure of the industry to expand, along with relatively high capital costs.[47] An American Physical Society Panel chaired by a former NRC chairman, and including another former NRC chairman and a former Under Secretary of Energy, concluded, in part, "there is a concern that the buildup of spent fuel at reactor sites and lack of progress on final disposition could be serious constraints on the growth of the domestic nuclear power industry by discouraging investment in new nuclear power plants and enhancing the difficulty of siting new nuclear power plants."[48]

A recent article by long-time nuclear waste observers and former officials argued that "solid public acceptance of nuclear energy ... may well turn on a credible promise of a geologic repository becoming available within the next few decades."[49] Another longtime observer of the nuclear industry indicated, "[e]ven if the public were otherwise prepared to go along with a major expansion of nuclear power, much less reprocessing, it is unlikely to do so without a new, credible regime for disposing of our existing and future nuclear power wastes."[50]

The recent report by the BRC also implicated the current "impasse" in the U.S. nuclear waste program as a hindrance to expansion of nuclear power, among other impacts:

> Put simply, this nation's failure to come to grips with the nuclear waste issue has already proved damaging and costly and it will be more damaging and more costly the longer it continues: damaging to prospects for maintaining a potentially important energy supply option for the future, damaging to state-federal relations and public confidence in the federal government's competence, and damaging to America's standing in the world—not only as a source of nuclear technology and policy expertise but as a leader on global issues of nuclear safety, non-proliferation, and security.[51]

States have imposed their own controls on SNF management and related nuclear power plant operations.[52] Specifically, some state laws prohibit construction of any new nuclear power plants until the current backlog of spent fuel is addressed. According to the National Conference of State Legislatures, "Thirteen states have laws prohibiting energy utilities from even considering adding

[46] American Physical Society Nuclear Energy Study Group, *Consolidated Interim Storage of Commercial Spent Nuclear Fuel: A Technical and Programmatic Assessment*, February 2007; Michael F. Hertz, Deputy Assistant Attorney General, Civil Division, Before the Committee on the Budget, U.S. House of Representatives, *Budgeting for Nuclear Waste Management*, presented on July 16, 2009; and Hertz, Michael F., U.S. Department of Justice, *Statement Before the Blue Ribbon Commission on America's Nuclear Future*, February 2, 2011.

[47] Frank von Hippel, *The Uncertain Future of Nuclear Energy*, International Panel on Fissile Materials Report #9, September 2010.

[48] American Physical Society Nuclear Energy Study Group, *Consolidated Interim Storage of Commercial Spent Nuclear Fuel: A Technical and Programmatic Assessment*, February 2007.

[49] Luther J. Carter, Lake H. Barrett, and Kenneth C. Rogers, "Nuclear Waste Disposal Showdown at Yucca Mountain," *Issues in Science and Technology* (Lawrence Livermore National Laboratory), Fall 2010.

[50] Richard B. Stewart and Jane B. Stewart, *Fuel Cycle to Nowhere: U.S. Law and Policy on Nuclear Waste* (Nashville, TN: Vanderbilt University Press, 2011).

[51] Blue Ribbon Commission on America's Nuclear Future, *Report to the Secretary of Energy*, January 26, 2012, p. vi.

[52] Richard C. Moore, *Enhancing the Role of State and Local Governments in America's Nuclear Future: An Idea Whose Time Has Come*, prepared for the Blue Ribbon Commission on America's Nuclear Future, May 2011.

new nuclear reactors until the waste problem has been solved."[53] State authority, however, is limited under the Atomic Energy Act.[54]

This report cannot resolve these issues, but it does provide some vital background to help support an informed debate on the issues of SNF storage.

# What Is Spent (Used) Fuel?

In many cases, discussions of "nuclear waste"[55] are, in fact, referring to SNF. The "fuel" in commercial nuclear fuel is uranium oxide[56] formed into solid cylindrical ceramic pellets, contained in zirconium alloy tubes supported in a rigid metal framework, or "assembly" (see **Figure 1**). These fuel assemblies are composed of individual rods of approximately half an inch in diameter and 12 to 15 feet long, with each assembly approximately 5 inches to 9 inches on a side.[57] The fuel assemblies for a boiling water reactor (BWR) are about half the mass (about 0.18 MTU/assembly) of a typical pressurized water reactor (PWR), which are about 0.44 MTU/assembly.[58] The difference in design of BWR and PWR reactors is significant in how SNF is stored, which is discussed below. Both types of reactors are "light water reactors" because they use ordinary ("light") water for cooling and reducing neutron energy.[59] All current U.S. commercial reactors are light water reactors.

---

[53] Savage, Melissa, "The Other Nuclear Problem," *State Legislatures Magazine* (National Conference of State Legislatures), May 2011 (see http://www.ncsl.org/?tabid=22533). Also, see CRS Report R41984, *State Authority to Regulate Nuclear Power: Federal Preemption Under the Atomic Energy Act (AEA)*, by Todd Garvey.

[54] See CRS Report R41984, *State Authority to Regulate Nuclear Power: Federal Preemption Under the Atomic Energy Act (AEA)*, by Todd Garvey.

[55] See CRS Report RL32163, *Radioactive Waste Streams: Waste Classification for Disposal*, by Anthony Andrews (2006), and out of print CRS Report RS22001, *Spent Nuclear Fuel Storage Locations and Inventory*, by Anthony Andrews (2004; available upon request).

[56] Uranium dioxide (UO2) is the most commonly used form of uranium used for fuel in commercial nuclear reactors, which is the focus of this report. Commercial reactor fuel uses uranium enriched to approximately 3%-5% U-235, with the balance of the uranium (approximately 95%-97%) U-238, which is "non-fissile," or incapable of sustaining a nuclear chain reaction. Other reactors for use in naval nuclear propulsion reactors, nuclear materials production reactors, and research applications may have different compositions in terms of uranium enrichment, overall structure, and cladding, but this report focuses on the typical fuel used in most commercial reactors. Some have proposed using thorium and/or metallic fuels (see, e.g., http://www.ltbridge.com) for "next generation" nuclear fuels.

[57] W. J. Bailey, A.B. Johnson, and D.E. Blahnik et al., *Surveillance of LWR Spent Fuel in Wet Storage*, Battelle Pacific Northwest Laboratories, Electric Power Research Institute Report NP-3765, October 1984.

[58] The mass per assembly is based on the average total discharge mass (metric tons of heavy metal, or MTHM) reported by the Energy Information Administration (EIA) for BWR and PWR reactors from 1968 to 1998, which was a period for which complete and comparable records were available at Energy Information Administration, Form RW-859, "Nuclear Fuel Data" (1998). The quantity of spent fuel is measured in MTHM. Heavy metal refers to elements with atomic number greater than 89—in SNF, almost all heavy metal is uranium. The mass generally refers to the initial heavy metal (i.e., before irradiation), and is roughly equivalent to the MTU. After discharge, some (about 4%) of the uranium has been replaced by fission products.

[59] Light water reactors are distinguished from heavy water reactors, which use deuterium oxide (D20) instead of H20. Like H20, D2O is composed of two hydrogen atoms and an oxygen atom, except the hydrogen atoms each possess an extra neutron.

---

**Figure 1. Nuclear Fuel Assembly**

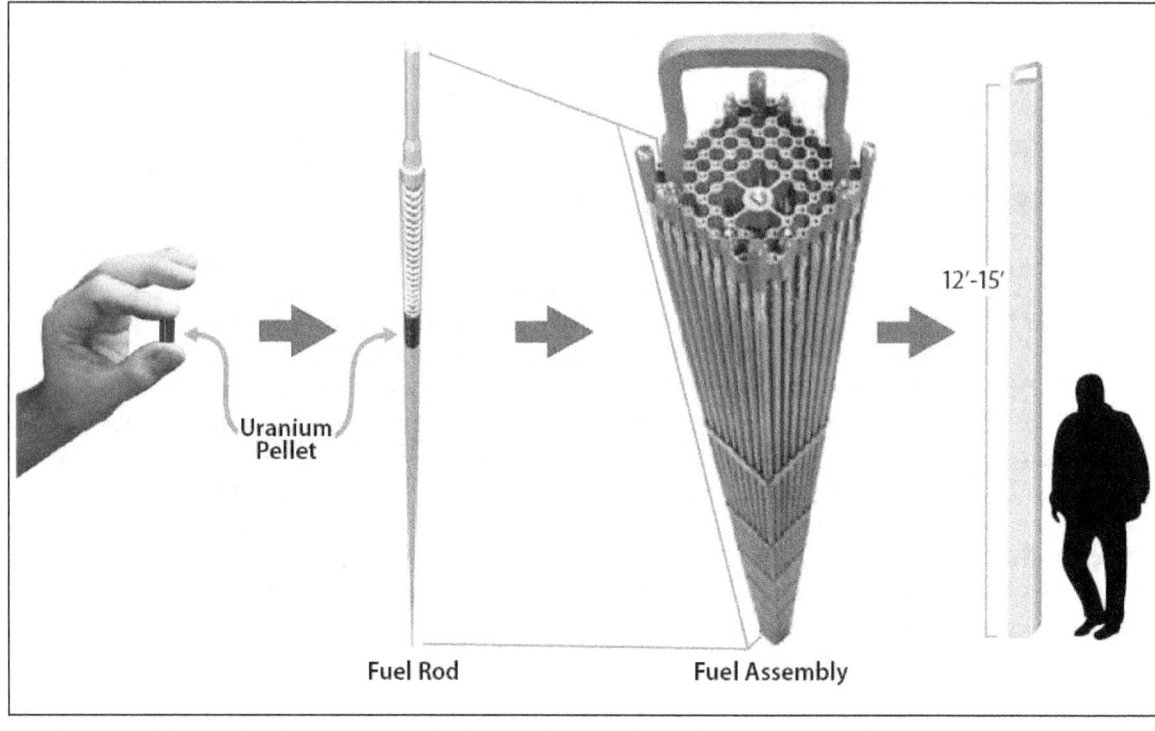

**Source:** CRS-produced graphic using SNF assembly image from General Electric Company.

**Note:** Illustrates a typical light water reactor nuclear fuel assembly used in U.S. commercial nuclear power reactors, and may not resemble fuel for research reactors, naval nuclear propulsion reactors, or nuclear power reactor fuel in other countries.

The production of electricity through nuclear fission in a light water reactor uses low-enriched uranium (3%-5% U-235) pellets that undergo a nuclear fission process inside the reactor. The fission process heats water to generate steam that turns the turbine generator, thereby generating electricity. In general, the fuel rods are productive for approximately 54 months. Roughly every 18 months, utilities generally conduct a refueling outage in which approximately one-third of the fuel assemblies are replaced with new assemblies. A replaced fuel assembly becomes spent (or "used") nuclear fuel when it has been irradiated and removed from a nuclear reactor after it is no longer cost-effective to generate power. This reduced power output is caused by the accumulation of radionuclides generated by the fission (splitting) of the uranium atoms and the relative reduction in fissile isotopes.[60] These fission products effectively "poison" the nuclear chain reaction by interfering with the otherwise self-sustaining fission process. The SNF assemblies must be removed to maintain the necessary power production level to generate electricity. A typical commercial nuclear power plant fuel rod assembly operates in a reactor for approximately 4½ years before being removed for storage and eventual disposal.[61] Once removed from the

---

[60] The relatively large uranium-235 atom splits into smaller fission products, with different radiological and chemical characteristics, such as cesium-137 (half-life (t1/2) = 30 years), strontium-90 (t1/2 = 29 years), and technecium-99 (t1/2 = 211,000 years). It is one of the fundamentally unique and remarkable characteristics of nuclear fission that it is capable of creating wholly new elements from others in a process that had previously eluded humans for centuries, since the days of the ancient alchemists.

[61] Some have suggested that "reprocessing" (dissolving of solid spent fuel rods in acid and using organic solvents to separate long-lived plutonium and uranium isotopes from certain fission products) could provide an alternative to spent fuel disposal. In the United States, most reprocessing was conducted from the 1940s until 1992 to extract plutonium (continued...)

reactor core, SNF continues to generate heat and radiation, and, although is rapidly attenuated, requires careful management for thousands of years. Commercial reactors in the United States generate about 2,000 MT of SNF annually.[62]

The variety of SNF types is as diverse as the range of reactors and their functions, which is dominated by, but not limited to, commercial nuclear power plants designed to produce electric power. This report is focused on commercial SNF, in contrast to smaller quantities of other types of SNF, which include SNF with different designs and characteristics from other sources:

- DOE production reactors used for producing nuclear materials, such as Pu-239 (weapons-grade plutonium) and Pu-238 (for deep space missions and other applications requiring durable power sources);[63]

- reactors used for research, analysis of materials, basic science experiments, and training;[64] and

- naval propulsion reactors used for submarines and aircraft carriers.[65] The Naval Nuclear Propulsion Program (i.e., nuclear submarines, aircraft carriers, and Navy prototype and training reactors) has generated about 27 MTU of SNF, which is stored at the Idaho National Laboratory.[66]

---

(...continued)

and other nuclear materials, primarily for nuclear weapons production. A complete examination of this technology is beyond the scope of this report and has been addressed in other CRS products. See, e.g., CRS Report RL34234, *Managing the Nuclear Fuel Cycle: Policy Implications of Expanding Global Access to Nuclear Power*, coordinated by Mary Beth Nikitin.

[62] The January 2011 NEI "Used Fuel" inventory report by Brian Gunterman estimated the average annual discharges of commercial SNF in the United States are slightly more than 2,000 MTHM (2,248 MTHM average annual rate for 2005-2010, and 2,259 MTHM average annual discharge rate projected for 2005-2025), but 2,000 MTHM is the estimated annual rate most commonly used in other analyses and is used here to provide comparability.

[63] The production reactors were all built by the former Atomic Energy Commission and the original Manhattan Project in World War II at the Hanford Site in eastern Washington and the Savannah River Plant in South Carolina. Instead of generating heat to drive a turbine to generate electricity, these reactors generally used high-enriched uranium fuel to irradiate targets to transmute U-238 into weapons-grade Pu-239. Although commercial reactors also produce Pu-239, theft of commercial SNF is not directly a significant proliferation risk because the concentration of Pu-239 is relatively low (compared to other plutonium isotopes). Perhaps more significantly, extracting the most useful plutonium isotope for efficient weapons (i.e., Pu-239) requires a much more challenging step of reprocessing to separate the Pu-239 from the fission products, which otherwise renders the fissile material useless for power or weapons, thereby making commercial SNF a low proliferation risk. Another difference with DOE production reactor SNF, compared to commercial SNF, is that the fuel cladding is relatively thin-walled to facilitate reprocessing by reducing the material that has to be dissolved. One reactor ("N-reactor" at the Hanford site) was built to produce both weapons material and electricity. Although it was built in the early 1960s as a potential model for other "dual use" reactors, it was never replicated and shut down in the 1980s.

[64] Research reactor fuel is generally smaller than commercial fuel (i.e., about 4 feet compared to 12 to 15 feet long). In many cases, research reactors used high-enriched or "weapons grade" uranium and posed a greater proliferation threat than low-enriched commercial fuel. DOE has operated a Reduced Enrichment Research and Test Reactor Program to help these reactors convert to high-density, low-enriched uranium fuel.

[65] The fuel used by the Naval Nuclear Propulsion Program has a significantly different and classified design from commercial, production, or research reactor fuel. Among other things, it uses high-enriched uranium and lasts considerably longer.

[66] Blue Ribbon Commission paper by DOE contractors, "Used Fuel Disposition: U.S. Radioactive Waste Inventory and Characteristics Related to Potential Future Nuclear Energy Systems," FCRD-USED-2011-000068, Rev. 18, May 2011.

---

Virtually all of this SNF is DOE-owned and comprises less than 4% of the amount of commercial SNF stored in the United States (2,458 MTU vs. 67,450 MTU). These noncommercial SNF types include a wide range of designs and sizes, which differ significantly from commercial reactor fuel, but share the same basic radioactivity hazard and need for long-term isolation. Many of the technical issues associated with long-term storage of commercial SNF also apply to these fuel types. This inventory of DOE-owned SNF does not include the millions of gallons of liquid high-level waste stored in underground tanks or the canisters of vitrified high-level waste resulting from reprocessing SNF at DOE sites.

## How Is Spent Fuel Stored Now?

There are essentially two modes of SNF storage in the United States: wet pools and dry casks.[67] Wet storage pools are the most common method for storing SNF in the United States, accounting for about 73% (49,338 MTU) of the current commercial SNF inventory. The remaining 27% (18,112 MTU) of commercial SNF is stored in dry casks on concrete pads or horizontal bunkers. Operating commercial nuclear power plants must store SNF at least a year (often five years or more) in "spent fuel pools" to allow for some initial cooling after discharge from the reactor. Because of limited wet storage capacity for SNF, most sites employ a combination of wet pool and dry cask storage. NRC regulates both wet fuel pools[68] and dry cask installations[69] and regards both as adequately protective (see "Options for Storing Spent Nuclear Fuel" below).

Wet storage pools are constructed of reinforced concrete walls several feet thick, with stainless steel liners. The water is typically about 40 feet deep, and serves both to shield workers from radiation and cool the SNF assemblies. Storage pools vary somewhat in size, but are generally large enough to store fuel rods vertically, with ample depth to provide space above the SNF storage racks for unloading and loading SNF transfer casks with SNF that is approximately 12 to 15 feet long. The cooling water chemistry is generally carefully controlled to minimize corrosion.

Just as the fuel assemblies' designs differ among different reactor types, described above, the designs of the pool storage basins differ significantly among different reactor designs, often unique to each plant. Currently, commercial nuclear reactors in the United States are light water reactors, of which there are two basic designs: boiling water reactors (BWRs; see **Figure 2**), and pressurized water reactors (PWRs; see **Figure 3**), the former being the type of reactor built at the Fukushima Dai-ichi site in Japan. Some SNF being stored in the United States, however, was

---

[67] Dry cask storage is sometimes considered synonymous with "Independent Spent Fuel Storage Installation" (ISFSI) because all but one ISFSI site (GE Morris in Illinois) uses dry casks. This report uses both terms where appropriate. Also, this report generally refers to typical commercial dry cask storage. In fact, a wide range of dry storage configurations are used, including vertical and horizontal configurations (see **Figure 4**), as well as in-ground and indoor vaults, which are used disproportionately at DOE sites.

[68] 10 C.F.R. Part 50.

[69] 10 C.F.R. Part 72.

generated by other reactor types[70] not currently used in this country, such as high temperature gas-cooled reactors and liquid sodium reactors.[71]

The design of storage pools has been highlighted recently for the GE Mark I BWR, which has been used at dozens of nuclear power plants worldwide, including the Fukushima Dai-ichi plant, as well as 20 reactors operating in the United States. The SNF storage pool for the GE Mark I reactor is approximately 35 feet wide, 40 feet long, and 39 feet deep (10.7 meters wide, 12.2 meters long, and 11.9 meters deep), with a water capacity of almost 400,000 gallons (1.51 million liters). Another feature of the GE Mark I BWR is that the SNF storage pool is located inside the same secondary containment structure as the reactor and many critical control systems. Finally, the SNF storage pools in the BWR Mark I reactors are located several stories above ground level. The potential safety considerations of these design features are discussed below in "Hazards and Potential Risks Associated with SNF Storage."

**Figure 2. SNF Storage Pool Location in Boiling Water Reactor**

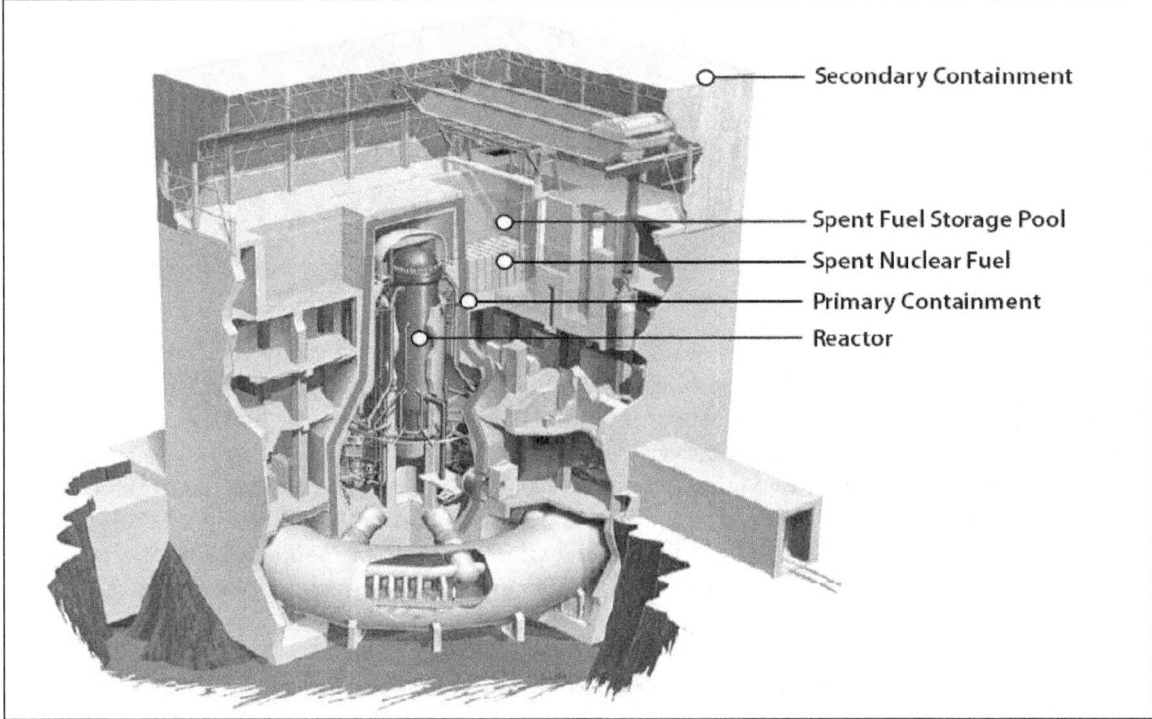

**Source:** GE-Hitachi Nuclear Energy.

**Note:** Illustrates a GE Mark I BWR design, which is one of a number of BWR designs.

---

[70] Other, generally noncommercial, reactors types have been used for nuclear materials production by the Department of Energy and predecessor agencies for nuclear weapons material production, and for research purposes. In addition, commercial reactors in the former Soviet Union have used other designs, such as the graphite reactor (known as a "RBMK" reactor) used at the Chernobyl plant in the Ukraine.

[71] The Fort St. Vrain facility in Colorado (25 MT and 2,208 assemblies of SNF stored on-site, while the balance was shipped off-site to DOE's Idaho National Engineering Laboratory) was a high temperature gas-cooled reactor. The Santa Susanna Field Laboratory in California and the Fermi 1 reactor in Michigan were liquid sodium reactors. In addition to this historic variation in reactor designs in the United States, reactor and fuel designs in other countries vary significantly. Canada, for example, has used "CANDU" reactors that use heavy water, and the British have used "Magnox" reactors, with relatively unstable fuel intended for relatively quick reprocessing.

---

## Figure 3. PWR SNF Storage Pool Location

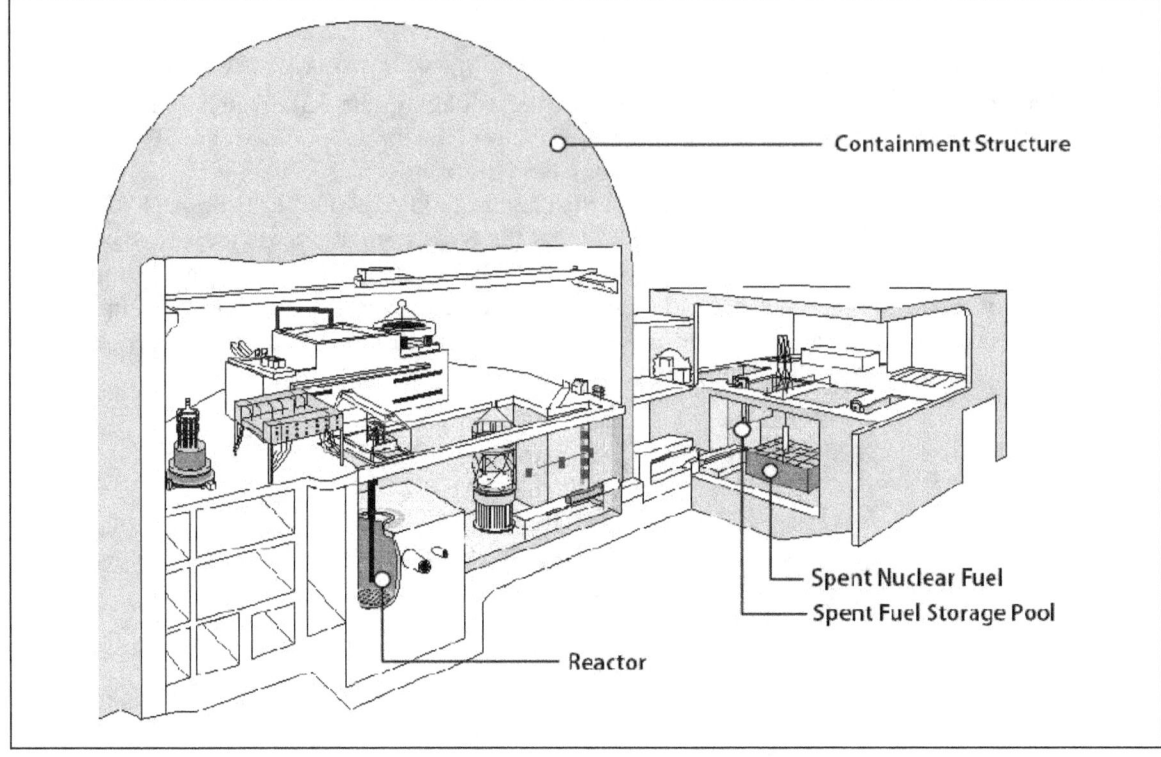

**Source:** Timothy Guzda, Union of Concerned Scientists, modified by CRS.

The SNF storage capacities using wet storage pools at U.S. commercial power reactors generally range from approximately 2,000 assemblies to 5,000 assemblies (averaging approximately 3,000 SNF fuel assemblies). Typically, U.S. spent fuel pools are filled with spent fuel assemblies up to approximately three-quarters of their capacity to allow space for at least one full reactor core load of fuel to be stored as needed. In contrast, the wet storage pool building located nearby but separate from the reactors at the Fukushima Dai-ichi site contains about 6,000 spent fuel assemblies, which was about half of the SNF at the site. U.S. reactor facilities do not typically have an additional spent fuel wet storage building for on-site SNF consolidation like that at Fukushima Dai-ichi.[72]

A critical feature of wet pools is the need for power to provide makeup water and circulate the water to keep it from boiling off and uncovering the fuel, especially for recently discharged SNF that is still thermally and radioactively hot. The SNF loses much of its heat in the first few weeks after discharge, and after five years produces relatively little thermal energy. Nonetheless, without circulation pumps helping remove the accumulated heat, the heat emitted from SNF can be sufficient to boil away the cooling water.

---

[72] The NRC Near-Term Task Force report in July 2011 put the number of assemblies in this basin at 6,291, while the INPO report from November 2011 indicated 6,375 assemblies were located in this separate storage pool. See U.S. NRC, *Recommendations for Enhancing Reactor Safety in the 21st Century: The Near-Term Task Force Review of Insights from the Fukushima Dai-ichi Accident*, July 12, 2011 (http://pbadupws nrc.gov/docs/ML1118/ML111861807.pdf); and Institute for Nuclear Power Operations, *Special Report on the Nuclear Accident at the Fukushima Daiichi Nuclear Power Station*, INPO 11-005, Rev. 0, November 2011, at page 35 (http://www.nei.org/resourcesandstats/documentlibrary/safetyandsecurity/reports/special-report-on-the-nuclear-accident-at-the-fukushima-daiichi-nuclear-power-station).

Dry casks are typically constructed in a cylindrical shape with an inner steel canister directly storing the SNF assemblies that is bolted or welded closed, in an outer concrete cask (see **Figure 4**). After loading with SNF, dry casks are stored outside[73] vertically on a purpose-built concrete pad, or horizontally in a concrete storage bunker. An individual SNF storage cask can weigh more than 100 MT (220,000 pounds) and be more than 15 feet long and 6 feet outside diameter.[74] One regularly used SNF storage container (the "NUHOMS 61BT") weighs 22 tons empty and 44 tons loaded with SNF.[75] The largest dry casks licensed for use in the United States can hold up to 40 PWR spent fuel assemblies or 68 BWR spent fuel assemblies. The Transportation, Aging, and Disposal (TAD) Canister System proposed by DOE can hold up to 21 PWR or 44 BWR spent fuel assemblies.[76] The storage capacity of a dry cask depends not only on size but also on the burn-up and age of the SNF fuel to be stored. There are more than 50 different types of dry casks produced by about a dozen manufacturers approved by NRC for general use in the United States.[77] NRC regulates dry cask storage systems at 10 C.F.R. 72, and with various guidance documents (e.g., NUREG-1536).

The key feature of dry storage units is that, once constructed, filled, and sealed, they require no power for circulation of cooling water and are generally regarded as "passively safe." Natural convection of air through the outer concrete shell of the storage system is sufficient to cool the steel containment canister inside without reliance on power for pumps or fans. By contrast, a wet storage pool system typically requires power for recirculation and/or makeup of cooling water. Loss of power for a wet pool storage system for more than a few days or weeks could cause water levels to drop to levels resulting in potential risks (e.g., inadequate shielding or exposure of SNF).[78] The robustness of dry cask storage was illustrated recently by the results of an August 2011 earthquake centered in Mineral, VA, near the North Anna nuclear power plant.[79] According to NRC, the earthquake caused movement of the SNF dry storage casks, weighing more than 100 tons, of approximately 1 to 4½ inches, and had no significant impact on the casks or the SNF.

---

[73] In contrast to the practice of storing SNF in dry casks on outdoor storage pads in the United States, Germany requires dry casks to be stored in hardened storage buildings. See Ulrich Alter (Federal Ministry for the Environment and Nuclear Safety), *Management of Radioactive Waste and Spent Fuel in Germany*, presentation to the IAEA Conference, May 31, 2010.

[74] IAEA, "Operation and Maintenance of Spent Fuel Storage and Transportation Casks/Containers," IAEA-TECDOC-1532, January 2007.

[75] See http://www.iaea.org/inis/collection/NCLCollectionStore/_Public/37/088/37088622.pdf.

[76] See "Safety & Security of Commercial Spent Nuclear Fuel Storage: Public Report," National Academies Press, Washington, DC (2006).

[77] See http://www.nrc.gov/waste/spent-fuel-storage/designs html.

[78] For example, the common SNF storage pool at the Fukushima site, in which about 60% of the SNF at the site was stored, was estimated to be capable of losing power for at least 30 days before it caused a concern. See Institute for Nuclear Power Operations, *Special Report on the Nuclear Accident at the Fukushima Daiichi Nuclear Power Station*, INPO 11-005, Rev. 0, November 2011, at page 35 (http://www nei.org/resourcesandstats/documentlibrary/safetyandsecurity/reports/special-report-on-the-nuclear-accident-at-the-fukushima-daiichi-nuclear-power-station.)

[79] See generally http://www.nrc.gov/info-finder/reactor/na1 html.

---

## Figure 4. Example of Dry Cask Storage

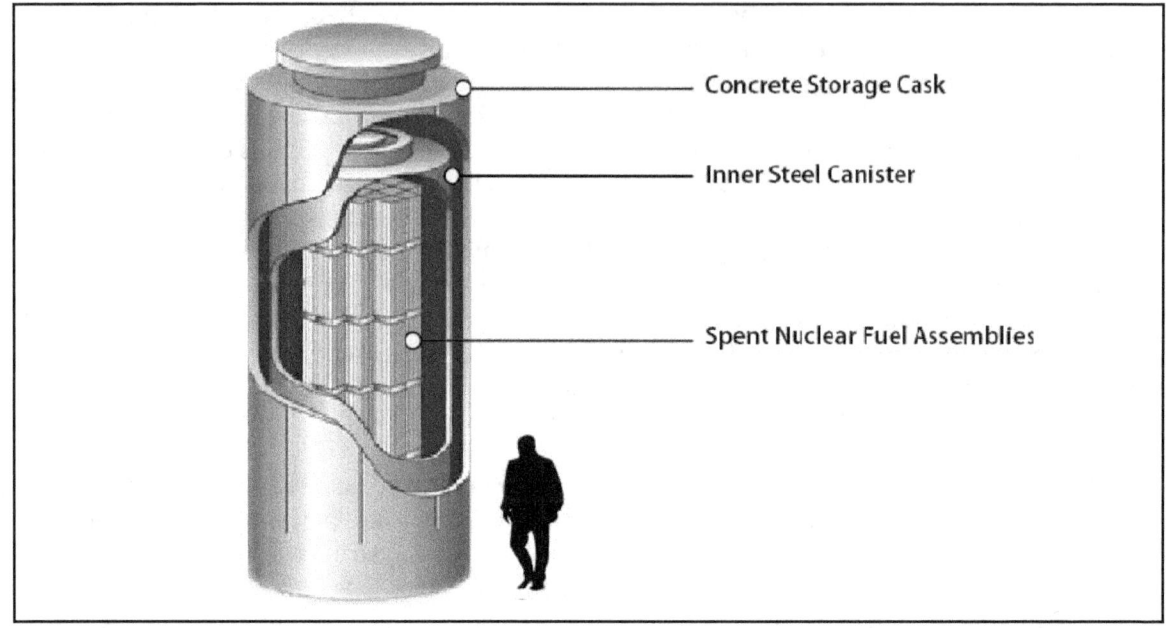

Concrete Storage Cask

Inner Steel Canister

Spent Nuclear Fuel Assemblies

**Source:** U.S. Nuclear Regulatory Commission.

**Note:** This figure illustrates a free-standing upright design. Other dry cask designs include horizontal and in-ground vaults.

NRC issues both general licenses and site-specific licenses for dry storage facilities.[82] A general license allows licensees to avoid repeating certain evaluations (e.g., National Environmental Policy Act or seismic review), if they have already been conducted pursuant to the plant operating licensing process. Part 72 contains NRC's regulations for the dry storage of power reactor spent fuel on or off a reactor site and for pool storage away from a reactor site. The NRC regulations have been adopted consistent with the International Convention on Nuclear Waste (see inset box).

> **International Nuclear Waste Convention**
>
> The United States is a party[80] to the Joint Convention on the Safety of Spent Fuel Management and on the Safety of Radioactive Waste Management.[81] The waste treaty includes provisions covering transboundary waste shipments, and facility planning, operations and closure, as well as requiring annual reports by each "Contracting Party." This treaty does not create any new obligations on U.S. SNF management, and provides a framework for a variety of strategies employed by a number of countries.

The first commercial dry SNF storage system in the United States was established at the North Anna nuclear power plant site in Virginia in 1986, and employs both vertical casks and horizontal modules.[83] Since then, an increasing number of storage locations have employed dry casks at an

---

[80] The United States signed the treaty on September 29, 1997, and ratified it on April 15, 2003. See http://www.iaea.org/Publications/Documents/Conventions/jointconv_status.pdf.

[81] International Atomic Energy Agency, *Joint Convention on the Safety of Spent Fuel Management and on the Safety of Radioactive Waste Management*, INFCIRC/546, December 24, 1997. See http://www.iaea.org/Publications/Documents/Infcircs/1997/infcirc546.pdf.

[82] 10 C.F.R. 72.2 and see U.S. NRC, "NRC Standard Review Plan for Dry Cask Storage Systems" (NUREG-1536).

[83] Two types of dry storage are used at the site: 27 vertical Areva/Transnuclear (TN)-32 metal casks and 26 TN NUHOMS HD-32PTH horizontal storage modules. See http://www.nrc.gov/about-nrc/emerg-preparedness/virginia-quake-info/north-anna-isfsi-summary.pdf; and Kenneth D. Kok, *Nuclear Engineering Handbook*, CRC press, 2009.

increasingly rapid rate. The amount of SNF transferred to dry cask storage in 2010 (8,606 assemblies) was nearly four times the average amount transferred since the use of dry cask storage began in 1986 (2,309 assemblies/year),[84] and was more than 50% greater than the assemblies transferred to dry casks in 2009.[85] The amount of SNF stored in wet pools compared to dry systems dropped from 91% (44,712 MTU/49,401 MTU) in 2002 to 73% (49,338 MTU/67,450 MTU) in 2011.

The amount of SNF stored in wet pools increased by about 10%, from 44,712 MTU in 2002 to 49,338 in December 2011, at an average annual rate of 437 MTU/year (1% average annual increase). The amount of SNF stored in dry systems increased during the same period by 286%, from 4,689 MTU to 18,112 MTU. The rate change in the amount of stored SNF reflected an average annual increase of total stored SNF of 1,579 MTU/year (3.2% average annual increase) and average increase in dry system storage of 1,124 MTU/year (24%/year average annual increase)—that is, storage of SNF in dry systems increased, on average, 24 times faster than storage in wet pools.

Regardless of government policies and requirements about SNF storage, it is likely that the trend toward more dry cask storage will continue because of the need for storage and the changing economic value, and extended pay-off period, of these investments given the long-term uncertainty about SNF disposal.

## Where Is Spent Nuclear Fuel Located Now in the United States?

Spent nuclear fuel is stored at 77 different sites[86] in the United States, including 63 sites with licensed operating commercial nuclear power reactors, 4 DOE-operated sites, 9 former operating nuclear reactor sites, and the Morris, IL, proposed reprocessing plant. Generally, the storage sites include facilities at the 104 licensed operating nuclear power reactor locations where it was generated (see **Table 1** and **Figure 5**), as well as 10 "stranded" commercial sites where no reactors operate (including the Morris, IL), and 4 DOE-operated facilities. In fact, virtually every site that has ever hosted a commercial nuclear reactor is currently also a storage site for SNF. As discussed above, because of practical, technical, and logistical limitations and other issues, SNF is likely to stay at existing sites for a significant period, regardless of decisions on a permanent

---

[84] Gutherman Technical Services (hereinafter referred to as the NEI Report), "2010 Used Fuel Data," Report to Nuclear Energy Institute (Marcus Nichol), January 18, 2010.

[85] ACI Nuclear Solutions (Brian Gutherman), Report to Nuclear Energy Institute (Everett Redmond), *2009 Used Fuel Data*, January 22, 2010.

[86] The term "sites" is used here to refer to geographically distinct locations. This accounting excludes the four sites where DOE is responsible for SNF storage in Colorado, Idaho, South Carolina, and Washington. Also, Hope Creek and Salem 1&2 (New Jersey) are counted as a single site because they are adjacent, located on the same artificial island in the Delaware River, share the same owner (PSEG Nuclear and Exelon), and share a dry cask storage pad using the same dry cask technology (Holtec Hi-Storm). An SNF storage "facility" is generally associated with a reactor that produced the SNF (see **Figure 2** and **Figure 3**), except in the case of the Morris, IL, facility, which was initially built not as a power reactor, but as part of an SNF reprocessing facility that never operated. In many cases there are more than one nuclear power reactor and SNF storage facility at a "site," which is a geographically contiguous area. Because dry cask storage areas are typically independent of a reactor facility at a site, and have a licensing process separate from the reactor licensing, dry cask storage is generally quantified according to number of sites, not facilities.

---

geologic repository. NRC has proposed plans that would consider SNF storage for up to 300 years, in the case of the oldest SNF now in storage.[87]

Of the 67,450 MTU[88] of commercial SNF stored in the United States, approximately three-quarters of it (49,338 MTU) is being stored in wet pools at the reactor sites. Of the 74 different sites[89] (some with multiple storage facilities) where commercial spent fuel is stored in the United States, 55 locations employ dry cask storage for at least part of the storage for commercial SNF.[90] There are 27 sites with 36 wet pool storage "facilities" (i.e., in some cases there are multiple wet pool storage "facilities" co-located at individual sites) where wet pool storage is the only technology being used at the site.[91]

---

[87] U.S. NRC, *Draft Report for Comment: Background and Preliminary Assumptions For an Environmental Impact Statement—Long-Term Waste Confidence Update*, December 2011, pp. 6-8 and 14.

[88] Excludes commercial SNF stored at DOE facilities.

[89] Includes the Hitachi-GE site in Morris, IL, but excludes the four DOE-operated sites.

[90] This number excludes three sites (Savannah River Site (SC) and Hanford (WA) and Fort St. Vrain (CO)) where DOE-owned SNF is stored in dry storage facilities. The Idaho National Laboratory (INL) DOE site is included because some of the SNF stored there is from the Three Mile Island reactor, and the dry storage facility at INL for the TMI SNF debris is NRC-licensed.

[91] Although the NEI data indicate it lacks a dry cask storage facility, the Salem (NJ) site is not included separately in this accounting because it is adjacent to the Hope Creek site and shares the dry cask storage facility there. Also, the Morris Site (IL) is included here because it is a wet storage site. In some databases, Morris is mistaken for dry casks because it is classified as an "Independent Spent Fuel Storage Installation (ISFSI)," which involves dry cask storage at all of the other ISFSI sites.

---

## Table 1. U.S. Spent Nuclear Fuel Storage Inventories by State (Ranked by Total SNF Mass)

As of December 31, 2011 (see **Table A-1** for data sorted by states alphabetically)

| State (15 states have no stored SNF)[a] | Number of Facilities | Number of Sites | "Stranded" SNF Storage Sites[b] | Mass (metric tons of uranium) | | | Assemblies | | | Table Notes |
|---|---|---|---|---|---|---|---|---|---|---|
| | | | | Wet Storage | Dry Cask | Total SNF | Wet Storage | Dry Cask | Total SNF | |
| Illinois | 15 | 8 | 2 | 6,900 | 1,791 | 8,691 | 28,242 | 9,625 | 37,867 | b & c |
| Pennsylvania | 9 | 5 | - | 4,606 | 1,459 | 6,065 | 20,898 | 8,424 | 29,322 | d |
| South Carolina | 8 | 5 | 1 | 2,236 | 1,808 | 4,044 | 5,001 | 3,896 | 8,897 | b & e |
| New York | 7 | 4 | - | 3,082 | 495 | 3,577 | 12,466 | 1,820 | 14,286 | b & f |
| North Carolina | 5 | 3 | - | 3,018 | 544 | 3,562 | 10,612 | 1,480 | 12,092 | |
| Alabama | 5 | 2 | - | 2,647 | 540 | 3,187 | 10,978 | 2,180 | 13,158 | |
| Florida | 5 | 3 | - | 2,511 | 445 | 2,956 | 5,859 | 1,024 | 6,883 | f |
| California | 7 | 4 | 2 | 2,017 | 916 | 2,933 | 4,750 | 2,486 | 7,236 | b & g |
| Georgia | 4 | 2 | - | 2,018 | 592 | 2,610 | 7,366 | 3,264 | 10,630 | |
| Michigan | 5 | 4 | 1 | 2,058 | 502 | 2,560 | 6,495 | 1,537 | 8,032 | b & f |
| New Jersey | 4 | 2 | - | 2,025 | 529 | 2,554 | 7,489 | 2,535 | 10,024 | h |
| Virginia | 4 | 4 | - | 970 | 1,477 | 2,447 | 2,120 | 3,229 | 5,349 | f |
| Texas | 4 | 2 | - | 2,121 | 0 | 2,121 | 4,522 | - | 4,522 | |
| Connecticut | 4 | 2 | 1 | 1,439 | 613 | 2,052 | 5,050 | 1,467 | 6,517 | b & g |
| Arizona | 3 | 1 | - | 1,052 | 903 | 1,955 | 2,490 | 2,136 | 4,626 | |
| Tennessee | 3 | 2 | - | 1,095 | 470 | 1,565 | 2,386 | 1,024 | 3,410 | |
| Maryland | 2 | 1 | - | 531 | 808 | 1,339 | 1,197 | 1,824 | 3,021 | f |
| Wisconsin | 4 | 3 | 1 | 915 | 419 | 1,334 | 2,603 | 1,088 | 3,691 | b & f |
| Arkansas | 2 | 1 | - | 607 | 726 | 1,333 | 1,336 | 1,600 | 2,936 | |
| Louisiana | 2 | 2 | - | 1,014 | 235 | 1,249 | 3,861 | 1,148 | 5,009 | |
| Minnesota | 3 | 2 | - | 678 | 525 | 1,203 | 2,645 | 1,770 | 4,415 | |
| Ohio | 2 | 2 | - | 1,083 | 34 | 1,117 | 4,542 | 72 | 4,614 | g |

| State (15 states have no stored SNF)[a] | Number of Facilities | Number of Sites | "Stranded" SNF Storage Sites[b] | Mass (metric tons of uranium) | | | Assemblies | | | Table Notes |
|---|---|---|---|---|---|---|---|---|---|---|
| | | | | Wet Storage | Dry Cask | Total SNF | Wet Storage | Dry Cask | Total SNF | |
| Nebraska | 2 | 2 | - | 650 | 203 | 853 | 2,825 | 808 | 3,633 | g |
| Mississippi | 1 | 1 | - | 602 | 203 | 805 | 3,428 | 1,156 | 4,584 | |
| Missouri | 1 | 1 | - | 679 | 0 | 679 | 1,696 | - | 1,696 | |
| Massachusetts | 2 | 2 | 1 | 542 | 122 | 664 | 3,082 | 533 | 3,615 | b |
| Washington | 2 | 2 | 1 | 319 | 339 | 658 | 1,715 | 1,836 | 3,551 | b |
| Kansas | 1 | 1 | - | 646 | 0 | 646 | 1,434 | - | 1,434 | |
| Vermont | 1 | 1 | - | 513 | 111 | 624 | 2,815 | 612 | 3,427 | |
| New Hampshire | 1 | 1 | - | 455 | 93 | 548 | 944 | 192 | 1,136 | |
| Maine | 1 | 1 | 1 | 0 | 542 | 542 | - | 1,438 | 1,438 | b |
| Iowa | 1 | 1 | - | 259 | 217 | 476 | 1,452 | 1,220 | 2,672 | |
| Oregon | 1 | 1 | 1 | 0 | 345 | 345 | - | 801 | 801 | b |
| Idaho | 1 | 1 | 1 | 50 | 81 | 131 | 144 | 177 | 321 | b |
| Colorado | 1 | 1 | 1 | 0 | 15 | 15 | - | 2,208 | 2,208 | b & f |
| U.S. Total Commercial Site Storage | 119 | 74 | 10 | 46,733 | 15,859 | 62,592 | 165,583 | 56,493 | 222,076 | |
| U.S. Total DOE Site Storage | 4 | 4 | 4 | 2,605 | 2,243 | 4,848 | 6,860 | 8,117 | 14,977 | |

**Source:** The primary source for these data is the Nuclear Energy Institute (NEI) report, "2011 Used Fuel Data," prepared by Gutherman Technical Associates, January 14, 2012. Site-specific data on sites with no operating reactors ("Storage-only Sites") is derived largely from DOE, *Report to Congress on the Demonstration of the Interim Storage of Spent Nuclear Fuel from Decommissioned Nuclear Power Reactor Sites*, DOE/RW-0596, December 2008. Data for DOE sites were generally from Frank Marcinowski, *Overview of DOE's Spent Nuclear Fuel & High Level Waste; Presentation to the Blue Ribbon Commission on America's Nuclear Future*, U.S. DOE, March 25, 2010.

a. There are currently 15 states with no commercial SNF storage (there may be temporary and relatively small-scale storage of SNF from non-power generating research and academic reactors): Alaska, Delaware, Hawaii, Indiana, Kentucky, Montana, Nevada, New Mexico, North Dakota, Oklahoma, Rhode Island, South Dakota, Utah, West Virginia, Wyoming.

b. "Stranded" is generally used to refer to SNF stored where the nuclear reactor that generated the SNF has ceased operating and been decommissioned, and the SNF remains at the site. In some cases the wet storage pools have been dismantled and the SNF is stored in dry casks. In the case of the Morris, IL, site, the "stranded" SNF was shipped from other reactor sites for a proposed reprocessing facility that never operated, and no reactor has ever operated at the site. The number of "stranded" SNF storage sites here does not include sites where SNF from decommissioned reactors is stored at sites co-located with operating reactors (e.g., San Onofre (CA), Dresden 1 (IL), or Indian Point (NY)). This table includes U.S. DOE facilities in Colorado, Idaho, South Carolina, and Washington that store commercial SNF, but where reactors have ceased operating, largely in the 1980s.

c.  Includes the Morris, IL, site, operated by GE-Hitachi, which never hosted an operating reactor or generated any SNF. The site was built to serve as an SNF reprocessing plant for which the SNF from other sites was shipped. The facility never operated, and the SNF has remained stored at the site. Many sources categorize the Morris site with dry cask storage sites, because they are all considered "Independent Spent Fuel Storage Installations" (ISFSI), although the Morris Site differs from other ISFSIs because it uses wet pool storage and is categorized accordingly here.

d.  Excludes SNF and debris generated at the Three Mile Island-2 facility removed after the 1979 incident and shipped to DOE's Idaho National Engineering Laboratory (now referred to as "Idaho National Laboratory").

e.  Includes 29 MTU of SNF, fragments, and nuclear materials stored at the Savannah River Site (SRS) near Aiken, which has been operated by DOE for nuclear weapons material production. In addition to material generated there, the SRS is used to store SNF shipped from commercial reactors (e.g., Carolinas-Virginia Tube Reactor) and from foreign and domestic research reactors using U.S.-origin fuel.

f.  Does not include SNF shipped to DOE federal facilities: 8 MTU from Florida, 1 MTU from Maryland, 12 MTU from Michigan, 16 MTU from New York, 22 MTU from Virginia, and 4 MTU from Wisconsin, as well as part of the SNF from the Fort St. Vrain site in Colorado, which was shipped to Idaho.

g.  Does not include SNF shipped to the Morris, IL, facility (see (b) above) from 4 states: 100 MTU from California, 34 MTU from Connecticut, 185 MTU from Minnesota, and 191 MTU from Nebraska. Includes 132 MTU shipped from other facilities in Illinois to the Morris facility.

h.  The adjacent Salem 1 and 2 and Hope Creek reactors share dry cask storage facilities and could be considered three facilities on a single contiguous site.

Sixty-three SNF storage sites also have operating commercial nuclear power reactors. At 10 commercial sites[92] and an additional four DOE-operated sites,[93] SNF is being stored where there is no operating reactor. At these "stranded" SNF storage sites, the nuclear reactors that generated the SNF have been shut down and at least partly decommissioned.[94] Virtually none of the SNF at these reactors has been moved from where it was generated to another site. In some cases, where reactors have been shut down and decommissioned, the SNF has been moved to another reactor site for storage. Most SNF storage is located in or near the operating nuclear reactor (or sister reactors) that originally generated the SNF (see **Table 1**).

The SNF storage at nine commercial sites where reactors have been shut down has warranted special attention by some in the nuclear industry, plant operators, utilities, and public service commissions monitoring costs. These stranded sites represent roughly half of the sites where reactors have shut down, but where SNF continues to be stored. Because these stranded sites do not share overhead costs (e.g., security, maintenance and utilities) with a larger operating reactor complex, the incremental storage costs are higher than at operating reactor sites.

At several other commercial sites (e.g., Millstone 1, CT; Dresden 1, IL; Indian Point 1, NY; and San Onofre, CA), SNF is stored at facilities where a reactor has ceased operating but other reactors at the same site continue operating.[95] In addition, SNF is stored at three DOE-owned sites where the reactors ceased operating.[96] At one commercial site in Colorado (Fort St. Vrain), the DOE operates an SNF storage facility from a reactor that shut down in 1989. More than 90% of the stranded commercial SNF is located at five sites. Where SNF remains stored in dry cask storage but no wet storage pool exists, there is some concern that this could make it difficult to repackage the SNF if the need arises because SNF transfers are generally done under water.

The Blue Ribbon Commission (BRC) concluded that the need to address this stranded SNF was one of "several compelling reasons to move as quickly as possible to develop safe, consolidated storage capacity on a regional or national basis," which it argued was "[t]he fundamental policy question for spent fuel storage."[97]

---

[92] Included nine former commercial reactor sites and the GE-Hitachi site in Morris, IL.

[93] The four DOE sites with long-term SNF storage are the Hanford Site (WA), Savannah River Site (SC), the Idaho National Laboratory (ID), and the Fort St. Vrain Site (CO). In addition, DOE has indicated that relatively small amounts of SNF (less than 50 kg at each) are stored at other sites including the Argonne National Laboratory (IL) and the Babcock and Wilcox facility in Lynchburg, VA. Also, several university research reactors temporarily store SNF. A total of about 3 MTU of SNF is stored at these various sites for which DOE provides support, away form the four main sites.

[94] One exception is the GE-Hitachi site in Morris, IL, which may be grouped with "stranded" sites, although it never hosted an operating nuclear reactor, but rather was intended for an SNF reprocessing plant (that never operated), for which the SNF was shipped.

[95] The term "stranded" is used to refer to situations where SNF is stored but the associated reactor is no longer operating and generating revenue to help pay for storage costs, despite the presence of associated reactors at the same site.

[96] In addition to the three former nuclear weapons material production facilities, DOE is also responsible for the storage of SNF located at the former Fort St. Vrain reactor site in Colorado, which now hosts a commercial natural gas power plant.

[97] Blue Ribbon Commission on America's Nuclear Future, *Report to the Secretary of Energy*, January 2012. http://brc.gov/sites/default/files/documents/brc_finalreport_jan2012.pdf. See page 35.

**Figure 5** shows generally that most of the SNF storage in the United States is located in the Midwest and on the East Coast. Specifically, measured by mass, more than 80% (54,092 MTU vs. 13,358 MTU) of SNF is stored at sites east of the Mississippi River. Measured by number of SNF assemblies, however, nearly 84% (197,002 assemblies) of the SNF is stored in eastern sites compared to approximately 17% (40,051 assemblies) stored in western sites.

**Figure 5. Spent Nuclear Fuel Storage Map**

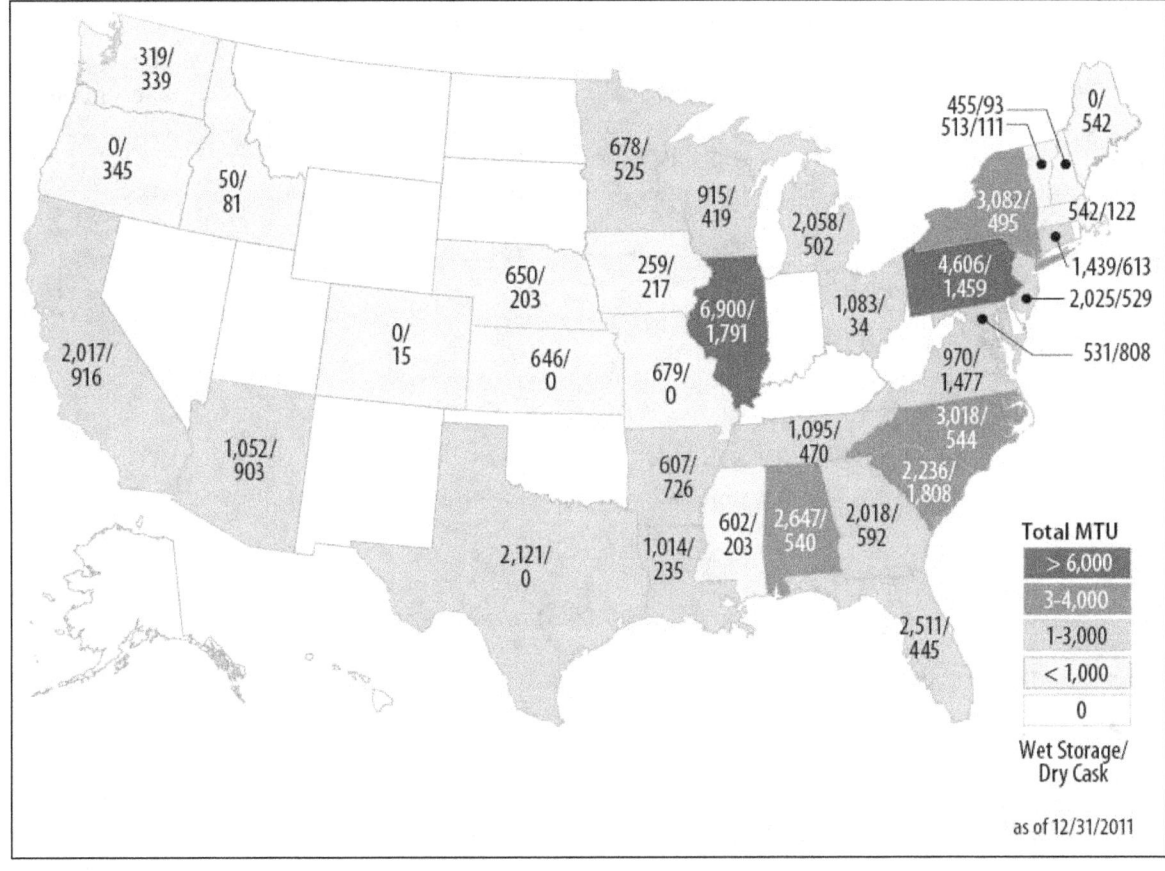

**Source:** Map prepared by CRS Graphics staff primarily using data from the Nuclear Energy Institute report "2011 Used Fuel Data," by Gutherman Technical Associates, January 14, 2012. See **Table 1** for more detail.

**Notes:** This map generally reflects storage quantities and location of commercial SNF, although relatively small quantities of commercial SNF are stored at U.S. DOE facilities. The map does not include SNF stored at U.S. DOE sites, which is a small portion (less than 4%) of total stored SNF.

The fact that BWR fuel assemblies are, individually, about half the mass of PWR fuel assemblies, combined with the fact that there are a disproportionate number of BWRs in the East compared with the overall number nationally,[98] helps explain why there is a greater share of SNF counted by assemblies, compared to the SNF mass (MTU), in the East.

---

[98] Approximately two-thirds of the nuclear power reactors built in the United States have been PWRs, while about one-third have been BWRs. A disproportionate number of the reactors built in the west (72%) were PWRs, whereas a somewhat larger percentage of the reactors built in the East were BWRs (36%). Approximately 80% of the total number of reactors built in the United States were built in the East, compared to about 25% in the West. Of the 40 BWRs built in the United States, more than 80% were in the East. Of the 76 PWRs built, however, about 75% were built in the eastern half of the United States.

Measured by mass of SNF, there is a slightly higher percentage (83%) of SNF stored in wet pools (40,260 out of 54,092 MTU) at eastern sites compared to the national share of SNF in wet storage (73%, or 49,338 out of 67,450 MTU). The corollary is that there is a somewhat disproportionate amount of SNF stored in dry casks at western sites (32%, or 4,280 out of 13,358 MTU) compared to the national distribution of about 27%.

Measured by number of assemblies, the disproportionate number of assemblies (86%, or 172,443 out of 237,053 assemblies) stored in wet pools in the East is greater than the share of wet pool storage at the western sites (15%, or 25,009 out of 40,051 assemblies), and greater than the national distribution (73%, or 172,443 out of 237,053 assemblies). It is not clear what accounts for this disproportionate share of SNF in dry cask storage at the western sites other than operator preference. Given the smaller size of BWR elements and the disproportionate share of BWRs located at eastern sites, however, it is predictable that the same disproportionate share of SNF by mass is amplified when measured by number of assemblies.

Measured by metric tons of heavy metal content (MTU), the five *states* with the largest *total* amount of SNF stored are

- Illinois (8,691 MTU),
- Pennsylvania (6,065 MTU),
- South Carolina (4,044 MTU; 4,073MTU with DOE SNF),
- New York (3,577 MTU),[99] and
- North Carolina (3,562 MTU).

The top five *states* with the largest amount (by MTU) of SNF stored in *wet pools* are

- Illinois (6,900 MTU),
- Pennsylvania (4,606 MTU),
- New York (3,082 MTU),
- North Carolina (3,018 MTU), and
- Alabama (2,647 MTU).

The top five *states* with the largest amount (by MTU) of SNF in dry storage systems are

- South Carolina (1,808 MTU),
- Illinois (1,791 MTU),
- Virginia (1,477 MTU),
- Pennsylvania (1,459 MTU), and
- California (916 MTU).

---

[99] Excludes two 132-liter drums of SNF stored at the West Valley site near Buffalo, NY. See Margaret Loop and Laurene Rowell, "Getting West Valley Demonstration Project Waste in the Right Path to Disposal," *Waste Management 2011*, February 27, 2011.

The rankings change somewhat if measured by the number of SNF assemblies depending on the portion of different types of reactors in each state (i.e., states with more BWRs have more assemblies per MTU than states with more PWRs).

Measured by number of SNF assemblies, the five *states* with the largest *total* amount of SNF stored are

- Illinois (37,867 assemblies),

- Pennsylvania (29,322 assemblies),

- New York (14,286 assemblies),

- Alabama (13,158 assemblies), and

- North Carolina (12,092 assemblies).

The top five *states* with the largest amount (by assemblies) of SNF stored in *wet pools* are

- Illinois (28,242 assemblies),

- Pennsylvania (20,898 assemblies),

- New York (12,466 assemblies),

- Alabama (10,978 assemblies), and

- North Carolina (10,612 assemblies).

The top five *states* with the largest amount (by assemblies) of SNF in dry storage systems are

- Illinois (9,625 assemblies),

- Pennsylvania (8,424 assemblies),

- South Carolina (3,896 assemblies),

- Georgia (3,264 assemblies), and

- Virginia (3,229 assemblies).

Generally, the total amount of SNF in storage increases by approximately 2,000 MTU per year in the United States, assuming current operation of about 104 commercial U.S. power reactors. The amount of SNF stored in dry casks versus wet pools reflects more year-to-year changes depending on decisions made by individual plant operators.

Historically, DOE and its predecessor agencies[100] accepted for storage and reprocessing significant amounts of spent nuclear fuel from commercial nuclear power plants. For example, DOE took possession of the spent fuel and debris from the 1979 Three Mile Island plant incident, and shipped it to a DOE facility in Idaho[101] as part of a "research and development" project. In addition, SNF was shipped to New York (West Valley) and Illinois (Morris), where the Atomic Energy Commission, a predecessor to DOE, was involved in reprocessing efforts. In the 1970s a relatively small amount (248.7 MTU) of commercial SNF was shipped from commercial reactors,

---

[100] Atomic Energy Commission and the Energy Research and Development Administration.

[101] The Idaho National Laboratory, known previously as the Idaho National Engineering Laboratory.

including utilities in Michigan and New York, to the West Valley site in New York,[102] which reprocessed SNF for about six years (1966 to 1972). The resulting high-level waste and contaminated facilities remain at the site. DOE has estimated that decommissioning and environmental remediation of the contamination at the West Valley site will continue until at least 2020, cost $3.7 billion, and require indefinite long-term stewardship thereafter.[103] The DOE sites in South Carolina and Idaho have also accepted relatively small amounts of SNF from research reactor SNF, some of which contains high-enriched uranium.

This report does not attempt to estimate the storage capacity of the existing facilities or sites. To do so would require judgments and determinations about the potential for and safety of re-racking SNF in more dense configurations that are beyond the scope of the analysis.

# SNF Management by the U.S. Department of Energy

The U.S. Department of Energy (DOE) has direct responsibility for storage of SNF and other reactor-irradiated nuclear materials at four sites: Fort St. Vrain (CO), Idaho National Laboratory (ID), Savannah River Site (SC), and Hanford Reservation (WA).[104] Because much of the DOE inventory includes material that is fundamentally different from commercial SNF (e.g., enrichment level/U-235 concentration, cladding, size, condition), it is not appropriate to list and sum these materials with commercial SNF.

A detailed description of this DOE-owned inventory is beyond the scope of this report, which is focused on commercial SNF stored at commercial sites. A brief summary, however, helps explain why it is accounted for separately in analyzing storage status issues and options. DOE and its predecessor agencies operated a number of nuclear reactors for weapons material production[105] and research. Although DOE ceased operating its large production reactors in the late 1980s and early 1990s, it continues to produce and accept SNF from research reactors. Much of the SNF from these reactors was reprocessed to extract certain nuclear materials (e.g., plutonium), which generated liquid high-level waste, which is intended, after processing, to be disposed of in a permanent geological repository with SNF. Some of DOE's SNF has not been reprocessed and remains stored as solid SNF.

In the case of the Savannah River Site (SRS), for example, there is a wide range of irradiated nuclear materials, including aluminum-based nuclear fuel, "higher actinide targets," and non-aluminum based fuel that DOE has characterized as "assemblies/items."[106] Like the SRS, the SNF

---

[102] U.S. DOE, *Spent Fuel Storage Requirements 1994-2042*, DOE/RW-0431-Rev.1, June 1995; and United States Court of Appeals for the District of Columbia Circuit, *State of New York, et al.; Petitioners, Nos. 11-1045, 11-1051, -against-11-1056, 11-1057 Nuclear Regulatory Commission, and United States of America, Respondents.*

[103] U.S. DOE, *The 1996 Baseline Environmental Management Report*, USDOE/EM-0290, June 1996.

[104] Frank Marcinowski, *Overview of DOE's Spent Nuclear Fuel & High Level Waste; Presentation to the Blue Ribbon Commission on America's Nuclear Future*, U.S. DOE, March 25, 2010.

[105] These reactors, and the nuclear driver fuel and target assemblies in them, were designed for production of nuclear materials including weapons grade (Pu-239) and other forms of plutonium (e.g., Pu-238 for durable power sources), tritium, and neptunium.

[106] U.S. DOE Idaho Office, Kathleen Hain, *Idaho Site Spent Nuclear Fuel; Management, Presentation to the Nuclear Waste Technical Review Board*, June 2010; U.S. DOE Inspector General Office of Audit Services, *Management of Spent Nuclear Fuel at the Savannah River Site* (DOE/IG-0727), May 2006; U.S. DOE, *Savannah River Site, Spent Nuclear Fuel Management Environmental Impact* Statement (DOE/EIS-0279), March 2000; and U.S. DOE (Dawn (continued...)

---

at DOE's Hanford site was largely surplus material from reactors used to produce materials (e.g., plutonium) for nuclear warheads, which was extracted using reprocessing facilities at the sites. The design of these fuel elements intended to be reprocessed for weapons material was different from commercial fuel elements (e.g., thin cladding). The Idaho inventory includes SNF from the Naval Nuclear Propulsion program (i.e., submarines and aircraft carriers), which is different from commercial SNF in multiple ways, including enrichment level and design. From about 1952 to 1992 this Navy SNF was reprocessed in Idaho to extract high-enriched uranium for use in driver rods at weapons material production reactors elsewhere.[107] The Idaho site is also home to the SNF debris from the partial meltdown of the Three Mile Island (PA) reactor in 1979. The DOE sites also store a variety of research reactor SNF—both foreign and domestic—that is often much smaller (e.g., 3 to 4 feet long vs. 12 to 15 feet long for commercial power reactor fuel) and more highly enriched than commercial reactor SNF. Some SNF stored at DOE sites came from commercially related activities, including commercial power reactors (e.g., Three Mile Island),[108] test reactors used for academic research (e.g., at 24 U.S. universities),[109] medical isotopes, and commercial power reactor research.[110] By the late 1980s, some of the SNF at DOE sites had become severely corroded or was stored in technically inadequate conditions. After 1993, DOE undertook a "Spent Fuels Vulnerabilities Assessment" and developed detailed "Materials in Inventory" plans to secure this material through packaging and processing, which have been partially implemented generally in conformance with recommendations of the Defense Nuclear Facilities Safety Board.

DOE-owned spent fuel includes some production reactor fuel, which has a fundamentally different design and construction from commercial spent fuel. This DOE-owned production reactor fuel generally has very thin cladding intended to facilitate reprocessing to recover plutonium or other nuclear materials. DOE, with recommendations of the Defense Nuclear Facilities Safety Board, has had a long-term plan to stabilize the relatively thin-walled DOE-owned SNF because it is less robust than commercial SNF, which has thicker and more corrosion-resistant cladding.[111]

The total amount of DOE-owned SNF and other reactor-irradiated material is about 198 MT, of which about half is stored in wet storage pools and the other half in various dry storage

---

(...continued)

Gillas), *SRS Used Nuclear Fuel Management: A Presentation to the Citizens Advisory Board*, July 2011.

[107] Thomas B. Cochran. Robert S. Norris, W. Arkin, and M. Hoenig (Natural Resources Defense Council), *Nuclear Weapons Databook, Vol. II, U.S. Nuclear Warhead Production*, Ballinger Publishing Company, Cambridge, MA, 1987. See http://docs.nrdc.org/nuclear/files/nuc_87010103a_65c.pdf.

[108] Largely core debris and damaged SNF from the Three Mile Island reactor. This was generally an exceptional situation, and most commercial reactor SNF is not sent to DOE facilities.

[109] Douglas Morrell, *DOE Research Reactor Infrastructure Program: 2011 Status Report*, September 14, 2011. See https://secure.inl.gov/TRTR2011/Presentations/Morrell_TRTR2011.pdf.

[110] For example, core debris resulting from the 1979 incident at the Three Mile Island-2 reactor in Pennsylvania, and commercial power demonstration projects at Shippingport and Peach Bottom in Pennsylvania, the Carolinas-Virginia Tube Reactor in South Carolina, Fort St. Vrain reactor in Colorado, and Sodium Reactor Experiment at the Santa Susanna Field Laboratory in California.

[111] Defense Nuclear Facilities Safety Board, "Review of the Hanford Spent Nuclear Fuel Project Defense Nuclear Facilities Safety Board," DNFSB/TECH-17, Technical Report, October 1997; Defense Nuclear Facilities Safety Board, "Technical Report: Stabilization of Deteriorating Mark 16 and Mark 22 Aluminum-Alloy Spent Nuclear Fuel at the Savannah Rover Site," DNFSB/TEC-7, June 1, 1995; and Defense Nuclear Facilities Safety Board, "Recommendation to the Secretary of Energy 94-1; Improved Schedule for Remediation of Nuclear Materials in the Defense Nuclear Facilities Complex," May 26, 1994.

configurations. All of the SNF at the Hanford and Fort St. Vrain sites has been transferred to dry casks, while all of the material at the SRS is stored in wet storage pools. The Idaho site employs both methods.

In addition to the different types of SNF and other reactor-irradiated material at DOE sites, DOE is also responsible for high-level waste (HLW) resulting from reprocessing of SNF. Hence, it could be misleading to simply sum the SNF at the DOE-owned sites with the SNF stored at commercial sites, possibly implying a total inventory of HLW intended for extended storage and eventual repository disposal. The SNF inventories at DOE sites must be accounted for separately from commercial sites to compile a meaningful assessment of the total inventory of HLW in the United States. At the Hanford site, the HLW remains stored in underground tanks (many of which have leaked into the ground) awaiting treatment. At the West Valley site in upstate New York, the HLW from SNF reprocessing has largely been vitrified into a borosolicate glass inside stainless steel canisters and awaits disposal. Some of the HLW at the SRS has been similarly treated on a larger scale. At the Idaho sites, the HLW from reprocessing of SNF is being stored in both a liquid form and a solid calcine form awaiting treatment to prepare for disposal. The details of HLW storage, treatment facility construction and operations, "waste incidental to reprocessing," glass log disposition, tank closure, and costs are beyond the scope of this report.[112]

Moreover, the exact inventory of SNF and irradiated materials at DOE sites is more variable than commercial SNF. In some cases DOE may use the SRS reprocessing "H-canyon," for which DOE is required by law to "maintain a high state of readiness"[113] to reprocess materials for recovery of nuclear materials or to stabilize materials for safety reasons.[114] DOE recently announced its intention to use the H-canyon to process plutonium non-pit scrap.[115] Although the exact inventory is difficult to compare because of qualitative differences, such as the non-pit scrap, it is useful to put in context the total SNF inventory at DOE sites to the overall totals. The 29 MTU of SNF at the Savannah River Site comprise about 1.2% of the DOE-owned SNF, and about 0.04% of the total SNF stored in the United States. After reprocessing, the SNF would be converted to a relatively small amount of fissile material, and a larger volume of liquid acidic radioactive waste containing much of the fission products. This liquid radioactive waste would be pumped into underground tanks and (minus any "Waste Incidental to Reprocessing")[116] ultimately processed into borosilicate glass logs inside stainless steel canisters destined for disposal in a permanent geological repository. The path forward for this material is beyond the scope of this report.

---

[112] See CRS Report RS21988, *Radioactive Tank Waste from the Past Production of Nuclear Weapons: Background and Issues for Congress*, by David M. Bearden and Anthony Andrews.

[113] FY 2001 Defense Authorization Act, P.L. 106-398, Section 3137.

[114] Defense Nuclear Facilities Safety Board, "Recommendation to the Secretary of Energy 94-1."

[115] DOE National Nuclear Security Administration, "Press Release: NNSA Announces H-Canyon to Support Plutonium Disposition at the Savannah River Site," October 31, 2011 (see http://nnsa.energy.gov/mediaroom/pressreleases/ hcanyon); and George Lobsenz, "NNSA to Process Plutonium for MOX at H Canyon," *Energy Daily*, November 2, 2011.

[116] See CRS Report RS21988, *Radioactive Tank Waste from the Past Production of Nuclear Weapons: Background and Issues for Congress*, by David M. Bearden and Anthony Andrews.

# Hazards and Potential Risks Associated with SNF Storage

Evaluating hazards and risks accurately and with sufficient precision is essential to making decisions about SNF management and regulation. The primary near-term hazard from SNF derives from the radioactivity from the decay of mixed fission products (e.g., cesium-137, strontium-90), and long-term hazards from plutonium and uranium. Hence, spent nuclear fuel generally poses a significant hazard but it may not pose a significant risk, depending on how it is managed. The distinction between "hazard" and "risk" is fundamental to analyzing the need for and benefits of various SNF management options. In classic risk assessment and toxicology, a hazard is the inherent potential of something to cause harm, whereas a risk is generally the product of a probability and the severity of an event (e.g., health, environmental, or financial impact). Whether a hazardous substance poses a risk depends on a variety of factors, including containment and exposure. For example, to the extent that spent fuel is effectively contained, the hazard can remain extremely high, but the risk may be low because there is no pathway for exposure.[117]

Regulation of SNF storage requires a consideration of risk, which involves characterizing the probability and consequence of potential threats. Regulation also requires a policy judgment about what level of assurance is warranted. Some would argue that the hazard, or consequence from the event, is so high that it demands a commensurately high level of protection, using any available technology, against threats to prevent any significant risks to human health and the environment.[118] Others, including a former NRC commissioner, have argued that the mandate of NRC is to "provide reasonable assurance of adequate protection, not absolute assurance of perfect protection."[119]

Although the thermal heat and radiation from SNF begins to drop as soon as the fission process ceases upon reactor shutdown, SNF assemblies continue to require cooling and shielding during storage after discharge from a reactor. Generally, SNF requires three to five years of wet pool storage before it has cooled enough for transfer to dry cask storage. While NRC has authorized transfer as early as three years, the industry norm is about 10 years. Some analysts and observers have expressed concern about the safety of current spent nuclear fuel management practices, at least for long-term storage methods.[120] Until the recently proposed termination of the Yucca Mountain repository project, however, these SNF storage methods were not generally considered "long-term."

---

[117] See National Academy of Sciences/National Research Council, "Risk Assessment in the Federal Government: Managing the Process," Committee on the Institutional Means for Assessment of Risks to Public Health, National Academy Press, Washington, DC, 1983; and Klaassen CD, Amdur MO, Doull J., *Casarett & Doull's Toxicology: The Basic Science of Poisons*, Macmillan Publishing (3rd Ed, 1986).

[118] Alvarez, Robert, *Spent Nuclear Fuel Pools in the U.S.: Reducing the Deadly Risks of Storage*, Institute for Policy Studies, May 2011.

[119] Wald, Matthew L., "Edward McGaffigan, 58, Atomic Official," *New York Times*, September 4, 2007. The term "adequate protection" is a term of art under Section 182 of the Atomic Energy Act of 1954. 42 U.S.C. 2232.

[120] Lisbeth Gronlund, David Lochbaum, and Edwin Lyman, *Nuclear power in a warming world; Assessing the Risks, Addressing the Challenges*, Union of Concerned Scientists, December 2007; Lochbaum, David, *Nuclear Waste Disposal Crisis*, Penn Well Books, Tulsa OK, 1996; *Newsday* Editorial, "Time to act on perilous piles; Memo to Congress: Do something now about our spent nuclear fuel," *Newsday*, April 22, 2011.

NRC and others have viewed SNF storage as a relatively safe operation, if reasonable precautions are exercised and normal conditions prevail. The inherent hazards of SNF, however, can result in a variety of risks under other conditions. A variety of forces or "threats" acting on spent fuel could result in containment being breached, resulting in potential exposures and risks, generally: (1) loss of power for water supply, circulation, or cooling, which can have significant consequences for SNF in wet pool storage;[121] (2) external threats, like hydrogen explosions from adjacent reactors, or an airplane crashing onto an SNF storage facility; (3) long-term degradation of SNF through chronic corrosion of cladding (e.g., hydride corrosion); and (4) leakage of contaminated water from wet pools to groundwater.

After the earthquake and tsunami in Japan, the first two of these concerns appeared to be occurring at the Fukushima Dai-ichi facility. In testimony on March 16, 2011, before a joint subcommittee hearing of the House Energy and Commerce Committee, NRC chairman Greg Jaczko stated that, following the hydrogen explosion at reactor #4 at the Fukushima Dai-ichi plant, there was an uncovering of the fuel in the pool and there was "no water in the pool."[122] A November 2011 report by the Institute for Nuclear Power Operations concluded that "[S]ubsequent analyses and inspections determined that the spent fuel pool water levels never dropped below the top of fuel in any spent fuel pool and that no significant fuel damage had occurred. Current investigation results indicate that any potential fuel damage may have been caused by debris from the reactor building explosions."[123]

Less than a week after the earthquake and tsunami, and two days after this testimony, NRC published a nonregulatory information notice to reactor operators to "review the information for applicability to their facilities and consider actions, as appropriate, to avoid similar problems."[124] This information notice reiterated NRC's process for adopting earlier Interim Compensatory Measures,[125] which dealt with spent fuel storage safety, among other issues. This initial NRC notice summarized the circumstances, indicating that "Units 3 and 4 have low spent fuel pool (SFP) water levels."[126]

A recent study by the Massachusetts Institute of Technology (MIT), soon after the Fukushima Dai-ichi incident, recommended that NRC and the nuclear power industry

> reexamine safety systems, operating procedures, regulatory oversight, emergency response plans, design basis threats, and spent fuel management protocols for operating U.S. reactors. Some of these issues were addressed in the aftermath of the TMI-2 accident and the

---

[121] After several years in pool storage, the thermal heat load from SNF drops significantly, and less heat removal from the water may be required. Nonetheless, the water continues to serve an important radiation shielding function.

[122] Jaczko, Honorable Greg, NRC Chairman, Statement before the Joint Hearing of the Subcommittee on Energy and Power and the Subcommittee on Environment and the Economy of the House Energy and Commerce Committee, "The FY2012 Department of Energy and Nuclear Regulatory Commission Budgets," March 16, 2011, http://energycommerce.house.gov/hearings/hearingdetail.aspx?NewsID=8329.

[123] Institute for Nuclear Power Operations, *Special Report on the Nuclear Accident at the Fukushima Daiichi Nuclear Power Station*, INPO 11-005, Rev. 0, November 2011, at page 35; http://www.nei.org/resourcesandstats/documentlibrary/safetyandsecurity/reports/special-report-on-the-nuclear-accident-at-the-fukushima-daiichi-nuclear-power-station.

[124] U.S. Nuclear Regulatory Commission, Information Notice 2011-05, *Tohoku-Taiheiyou-Oki Earthquake Effects on Japanese Nuclear Power Plants*, March 18, 2011.

[125] U.S. NRC, "Order for Interim Safeguards and Security Compensatory Measures," EA-02-026, February 25, 2002 (designated Safeguards Information, protected as "Official Use Only-Security Related Information").

[126] Ibid.

---

September 11 World Trade Center attacks, resulting both in hardening of U.S. nuclear plants against a number of accident scenarios and in improved emergency response preparations.[127]

The Government Accountability Office has recommended DOE "[a]ssess the condition of existing storage facilities and identify any gaps and actions that might be needed to address long-term storage requirements."[128]

In the wake of the Fukushima Dai-ichi incident, NRC dispatched inspectors to each U.S. reactor and SNF storage site. The results of these inspections varied with different sites, with NRC inspections revealing no significant vulnerabilities for most sites. For sites with the oldest SNF (e.g., at the GE-Hitachi Morris storage site in Illinois), the predicted impact of an extended loss of power to the site would be minimal because of the extent of the radioactive decay during the decades of storage. NRC predicted that, "in the unlikely event that the [spent fuel wet storage basin] is completely drained of water, fuel melt would not occur given the limited fuel decay heat load."[129]

The Fukushima Dai-ichi incident raised concerns about possible risks to SNF storage, including physical damage and loss of power. Although details remain unclear, the dramatic gas explosions that caused some of the overhead containment structure to collapse down into the pool appeared to have caused little or no damage to the SNF in the pools.[130] Also, despite the loss of power over an extended period and some loss of cooling water, the SNF in the storage pools appeared to have remained covered in water largely undamaged.

Notwithstanding these initial results on the SNF condition at the Fukushima Dai-ichi site, some analysts are concerned that, under some circumstances, SNF zirconium cladding can catch fire if left uncovered in wet storage pools. The National Academies/National Research Council concluded, based primarily on review of NRC studies,[131] "that a loss-of-pool-coolant event could trigger a zirconium cladding fire in the exposed spent fuel," but considered "such an accident ... so unlikely that no specific action was warranted."[132] NRC has issued a series of orders and letters to licensees to implement additional mitigation measures to address the issue.[133] NRC and others, including the nuclear industry, believe these actions provide reasonable assurance of adequate protection. Others disagree, including a long-time nuclear critic who has argued that the large inventory of radioactive material in wet pools poses a significant risk if the SNF pools were

---

[127] Massachusetts Institute of Technology, *The Future of the Nuclear Fuel Cycle: An Interdisciplinary MIT Study*, MIT, Cambridge, MA, 2011.

[128] U.S. Government Accountability Office, *DOE Nuclear Waste: Better Information Needed on Waste Storage at DOE Sites as a Result of Yucca Mountain Shutdown*, GAO-11-230, March 2011.

[129] Lipa, Christine A., U.S. NRC, NRC Inspection Report No. 072-00001/11-01(Dnms)—General Electric-Hitachi Morris, Letter to Mark Varno, GE-Hitachi Global Laser Enrichment, LLC, May 13, 2011.

[130] Institute for Nuclear Power Operations, "Special Report on the Nuclear Accident at the Fukushima Daiichi Nuclear Power Station," INPO 11-005, Rev. 0, November 2011, at page 35 (http://www.nei.org/resourcesandstats/documentlibrary/safetyandsecurity/reports/special-report-on-the-nuclear-accident-at-the-fukushima-daiichi-nuclear-power-station.)

[131] For example, see U.S. NRC, Technical Study of Spent Fuel Pool Accident Risk at Decommissioning Nuclear Power Plants, NUREG-1738, 2001.

[132] National Academy of Sciences, National Research Council, *Safety and Security of Commercial Spent Nuclear Fuel Storage: Public Report*, National Academies Press 2006 (based on classified July 2004 report to Congress), at page 44.

[133] Letter from Nils Diaz, Commissioner, U.S. NRC to Senator Pete Domenici, with accompanying report: U.S. Nuclear Regulatory Commission, *Report to Congress on the National Academy of Sciences Study on the Safety and Security of Commercial Spent Nuclear Fuel Storage*, March 14, 2005.

---

drained of water, the SNF were uncovered, and there was a release from an incident such as a fire or deliberate attack.[134]

The locations of SNF wet pool storage in relation to the associated nuclear reactor may present potential risks associated with those designs. For example, most boiling water reactors (BWRs) in the United States, including the GE Mark I, are designed with the SNF storage pool located inside the same secondary containment structure as the reactor and many critical control systems, and located well above ground level. Many have expressed concern that this design may pose safety risks because any problems with the reactor can affect the SNF storage pools, and vice versa.[135] For example, in a loss of off-site power situation, such as occurred at the GE Mark I reactors in Fukushima, Japan, the SNF pool may also lose power, affecting the cooling water and monitoring systems. In the case of the incident in Japan, elevated radiation near the reactor hindered personnel from mitigating problems or monitoring the SNF storage pools. In addition, the height of the SNF pools in many BWRs (more than 100 feet above ground level) could also pose safety risks because of the elevated access challenge and potential for a loss of coolant in a structural failure, compared to reactors with the SNF storage pools at or below ground level.

Prior to the Fukushima Dai-ichi incident, the biggest change in the risk profile for SNF storage occurred in the wake of the September 11, 2001, terrorist attacks, after which a congressionally mandated National Academy of Sciences report concluded that "attacks with civilian aircraft remain a credible threat."[136] NAS indicated that terrorists might choose to attack spent nuclear fuel pools because they are "less well protected structurally than reactor cores" and "typically contain inventories of medium- and long-lived radionuclides that are several times greater than those contained in reactor cores."[137] In response, NRC issued a series of orders and letters to licensees, the contents of which are confidential. NRC also conducted site-specific evaluations to review individual site risks and readiness, resulting in site modifications, the details of which are also confidential. Although the reviews, orders, and letters resulted in numerous incremental improvements to SNF storage facilities and operations, such as improved backup power supply reliability, there was no large-scale shift of SNF out of wet pools and into dry casks, nor was there a mandate to move SNF into hardened storage facilities.

By contrast, Germany explicitly requires protection against risks, including "external events" such as an attack on SNF storage,[138] and this has resulted in construction of hardened storage buildings for dry cask storage of SNF.[139] The Germans have also moved to establish consolidated central SNF storage facilities in the wake of a 2005 decision to cease reprocessing, and the lack of a geological repository.[140]

---

[134] Robert Alvarez, *Spent Nuclear Fuel Pools in the U.S.: Reducing the Deadly Risks of Storage*, Institute for Policy Studies, May 2011.

[135] David Lochbaum, *Nuclear Waste Disposal Crisis* (Penn Well Books, Tulsa OK, 1996); *Newsday* Editorial, "Time to act on perilous piles; Memo to Congress: Do something now about our spent nuclear fuel," *Newsday*, April 22, 2011.

[136] National Academy of Sciences, National Research Council, *Safety and Security of Commercial Spent Nuclear fuel Storage: Public Report* (2006), E725-846.

[137] Ibid. at 36.

[138] Section 6 para. 2 no. 4 (German) Atomic Energy Act.

[139] Ulrich Alter (Federal Ministry for the Environment and Nuclear Safety), *Management of Radioactive Waste and Spent Fuel in Germany*, presentation to the IAEA Conference, May 31, 2010.

[140] Jussofie, A., R. Graf, W. Filbert, German Approach to Spent Fuel Management, "IAEA-CN-184/30, 2010.z; and Harold Feiveson, Zia Mian, M. V. Ramana, and Frank von Hippel, "Managing Nuclear Spent Fuel: Policy Lessons (continued...)

Another potential threat to SNF storage safety is degradation of the cladding[141] and fuel elements. The potential for degradation of SNF cladding has been well known for decades, and the water chemistry of SNF storage pools is carefully controlled in part to protect against it.[142] The potential vulnerability of SNF varies with the particular type of fuel rod. Generally, however, the rate of corrosion and embrittlement of typical U.S. light water reactor zircalloy-clad commercial fuel rods is less than the rate for the British Magnox fuel rods, or DOE nuclear materials production reactor fuel elements, which are intended for shorter periods inside the reactor.[143] Hence, although some have expressed concern that U.S. nuclear fuel was not designed for long-term storage,[144] U.S. power reactor fuel has generally proven more durable than other fuel forms.

NRC concluded in its initial 1984 waste confidence rule "that the cladding which encases spent fuel is highly resistant to failure under pool storage conditions," and that "[c]orrosion studies of irradiated fuel at 20 reactor pools in the United States suggest that there is no detectable degradation of zircalloy cladding."[145] Nonetheless, BRC and NAS, among others, have recommended long-term research projects to evaluate the integrity of stored SNF,[146] such as ongoing work by the Electric Power Research Institute (EPRI).[147]

NRC has concluded that dry cask storage provides additional confidence in long-term storage of SNF:

> As long as the canister or cask has been properly dried and inerted, and the fuel temperature is kept within the limits of [NRC] guidance, there should be no active degradation mechanisms. The dryness is assured by following the proper drying procedure. No monitoring of the dryness is conducted. The canister is backfilled with an inert gas such as helium. The integrity of the closure seals is actively monitored. If there is indication that the closure seal is compromised, remedial action is taken. The issue of cladding integrity is being reevaluated as part of our extended storage and transportation review and all potential

---

(...continued)

from a 10-country Study," *Bulletin of the Atomic Scientists*, June 27, 2011.

[141] "Cladding" is the zirconium alloy metal tube in which the ceramic uranium oxide fuel pellets are encased to make a fuel rod.

[142] "Zirconium has a high affinity for hydrogen. Absorption of hydrogen leads to hydrogen embrittlement, which can lead to failure of the zirconium tubing used as cladding for nuclear fuel. In addition, zirconium also reacts with oxygen, which can lead to corrosion." From Kenneth D. Kok, Nuclear Engineering Handbook (CRC press, 2009), p. 287. Also, see W. L. Hurt, K. M. Moore, E. L. Shaber, and R. E. Mizia, Extended Storage for Research and Test Reactor Spent Fuel for 2006 and Beyond, IAEA Conference on Extended Storage of Research Reactor Fuel, October 14, 1999– October 17, 1999, INEEL/CON-99-01083.

[143] The design of the fuel elements for U.S. commercial power reactors was fundamentally different from nuclear materials production reactors (e.g., Hanford and Savannah River sites plutonium production reactors), which involve high-enriched driver fuel surrounded by "target" billets with relatively thin-walled cladding to facilitate reprocessing to extract the plutonium or other nuclear materials. See U.S. DOE, *Linking Legacies*, DOE/EM-319, January 1997. Some have argued that British Magnox reactor fuel was also not designed for long-term storage. Others have argued that U.S. commercial fuels were also not designed for long-term storage and that the difference is more one of degree than of kind.

[144] Massachusetts Institute of Technology, *The Future of the Nuclear Fuel Cycle: An Interdisciplinary MIT Study*, MIT Press, Cambridge, MA, 2011.

[145] 49 *Federal Register* 34658 (August 31, 1984).

[146] Blue Ribbon Commission on America's Nuclear Future, *Report to the Secretary of Energy*, January 26, 2012, p. 89.

[147] EPRI, *Used Fuel and High-Level Radioactive Waste Extended Storage Collaboration Program: November 2009 Workshop Proceedings*, March 10, 2010; and Kessler, J., EPRI, *Technical Bases for Extended Dry Storage of Spent Nuclear Fuel*, 1003416 Final Report, December 2002.

---

mechanisms for cladding and fuel degradation, even those analyzed to be inactive in the short term, are being reanalyzed for the potential to be active in the longer term.[148]

Finally, NRC has identified releases of tritium-contaminated water to groundwater at 38 sites,[149] and determined that, in some cases,[150] SNF storage pools had contributed[151] to groundwater contamination.[152] In addition to these commercial sites, tritium contamination was found in groundwater from spent fuel storage pools at DOE sites, including the Brookhaven National Laboratory in New York, Hanford in Washington State, and the Savannah River Site in South Carolina.[153] Evidence of groundwater contamination from leaking spent fuel storage pools was among the concerns cited by New York State in its objection to NRC's December 2010 Waste Confidence Rule. Tritium is inherently difficult to remediate, once released, because it is simply a radioactive form of hydrogen that substitutes freely with hydrogen in water and decays at a rate of about 5% per year (12.32 year half life). To address this issue, NRC in March 2010 established a Tritium Contamination Task Force. Notwithstanding these documented releases of radioactivity from stored SNF, there is no evidence of any resulting significant public exposures or health impacts. Nonetheless, concerns about contamination of groundwater from leaking SNF storage pools were among the issues raised by petitioners challenging NRC's "Waste Confidence Rule." In the wake of these findings, and NRC's own reviews, NRC has issued instructions to licensees and established releases to groundwater as a significant performance indicator, in addition to industry guidance on release prevention and reporting.[154] NRC has argued that these issues presented no public health or environmental risks, and that subsequent "Regulatory Guides," together with inspections, review of license applications, and industry forums and initiatives, will help prevent recurrence.[155] The litigation is ongoing.

NRC's "Waste Confidence Rule" arose from an effort to address the variety of concerns about spent fuel storage in a systematic and explicit manner, and to prevent them from being raised on a site-by-site basis as an issue during individual reactor licensing proceedings. Partly in response to a legal challenge and subsequent remand,[156] NRC issued in 1984 the first of three "Waste

---

[148] Personal e-mail from NRC staff (via Jenny Weil) to CRS, July 26, 2011.

[149] U.S. NRC, *List of Historical Leaks and Spills at U.S. Commercial Nuclear Power Plants*, Rev. 7, June 14, 2011. See http://pbadupws nrc.gov/docs/ML1012/ML101270439.pdf.

[150] In the case of widely reported tritium contamination of groundwater at the Vermont Yankee plant, the tritium release was determined to be from underground piping conduit leaks, not SNF storage.

[151] SNF storage pools were found to be one of a number of sources of leaks, including underground piping, valves on effluent discharge lines, leakage of components, and operator actions, which have caused several inadvertent releases. U.S. NRC, *Liquid Radioactive Release—Lessons Learned Task Force Final Report*, September 1, 2006, http://pbadupws nrc.gov/docs/ML0626/ML062650312.pdf; see page 3.

[152] U.S. Nuclear Regulatory Commission, *NRC Groundwater Task Force Final Report*, June 2010. See http://pbadupws nrc.gov/docs/ML1016/ML101680435.pdf.

[153] U.S General Accounting Office, *Information on the Tritium Leaks and the Contractor Dismissal at the Brookhaven National Laboratory*, GAO-RCED-98-26 (1998), and U.S. DOE, *The 1996 Baseline Environmental Management Report*, DOE/EM-0290, 1996.

[154] Nuclear Energy Institute Tritium Monitoring web page, "Fact Sheet: Industry Closely Monitors, Controls Tritium at Nuclear Power Plants," June 2009, http://www nei.org/resourcesandstats/documentlibrary/safetyandsecurity/factsheet/industrycloselymonitorscontrolstritium/.

[155] U.S. NRC, Regulatory Guide 4.1, "Radiological Environmental Monitoring for Nuclear Power Plants, Rev. 2" (June 2009, Rev. 2), http://pbadupws.nrc.gov/docs/ML0913/ML091310141.pdf, and Regulatory Guide 1.21, "Measuring, Evaluating, and Reporting Radioactive Material In Liquid And Gaseous Effluents and Solid Waste, Rev. 2" (June 2009), http://pbadupws.nrc.gov/docs/ML0911/ML091170109.pdf.

[156] *NRDC v. NRC*, 582 F.2d 166 (2d Cir. 1978) and *State of Minnesota v. NRC*, 602 F.2d 412 (D.C. Cir. 1979).

Confidence Decisions"[157] that included a series of specific findings, indicating generally that SNF could be stored safely at least until an expected geologic repository began operation to accept wastes. In the first two waste confidence rules, NRC identified a specific date by which a permanent repository would be available and until which SNF could be safely stored.[158] NRC's most recent revision of the rule, however, "removed a date when a repository would be expected to be available for long-term disposal of spent fuel."[159] NRC indicated that SNF could be stored for at least 60 years beyond the end of the reactor operating life:[160]

> The [NRC] has made a generic determination that, if necessary, spent fuel generated in any reactor can be stored safely and without significant environmental impacts for at least 60 years beyond the licensed life for operation (which may include the term of a revised or renewed license) of that reactor in a combination of storage in its spent fuel storage basin and at either onsite or offsite independent spent fuel storage installations.[161]

The nuclear power industry has indicated it "is confident that existing dry cask storage technology, coupled with aging management programs already in place, is sufficient to sustain dry cask storage for at least 100 years at reactors and central interim storage."[162]

Aside from the general assurance by NRC about the safety of the SNF storage, one of the implications of the waste confidence determination is

> no discussion of any environmental impact of spent fuel storage in reactor facility storage pools or independent spent fuel storage installations (ISFSI) for the period following the term of the reactor operating license or amendment, reactor combined license or amendment, or initial ISFSI license or amendment for which application is made, is required in any environmental report, environmental impact statement, environmental assessment, or other analysis prepared in connection with the issuance or amendment of an operating license for a nuclear power reactor.[163]

---

[157] First waste confidence rule (1984): 49 *Federal Register* 34658 (August 31, 1984). NRC also amended 10 C.F.R. 51.23(a) to reflect this determination. Second waste confidence rule (1990): 55 *Federal Register* 38474 (September 18, 1990). Third waste confidence rule (2010): U.S. Nuclear Regulatory Commission, "Consideration of Environmental Impacts of Temporary Storage of Spent Fuel After Cessation of Reactor Operations; Waste Confidence Decision Update; Final Rule," 75 *Federal Register* 81032, December 23, 2010. NRC also amended 10 C.F.R. 51.23(a) to reflect this determination.

[158] NRC's first (1984) waste confidence rule predicted that "one or more repositories for commercial high-level radioactive waste and spent fuel will be available by the years 2007-2008." This determination was based in part on DOE's projection that the first repository would be available in 1998 and the second repository would open by 2004 (See DOE, Attachment to May 21, 1984 Letter from J. William Bennett, DOE to Robert W. Browning, NRC, *"Draft Mission Plan,"* April 1984. NRC's second (1990) waste confidence rule predicted "at least one mined geologic repository will be available within the first quarter of the twenty-first century...."

[159] U.S. NRC, Tison Campbell, NRC Attorney, "A Level of Confidence," February 17, 2011, http://public-blog nrc-gateway.gov/2011/02/17/a-level-of-confidence/.

[160] In many cases this results in 120 years of expected safe storage if this 60 years (after the reactor operating period) is added to 60 years of storage while the reactor is operating.

[161] 10 C.F.R. 51.23 (a), and U.S. Nuclear Regulatory Commission, "Consideration of Environmental Impacts of Temporary Storage of Spent Fuel After Cessation of Reactor Operations; Waste Confidence Decision Update; Final Rule," 75 *Federal Register* 81032, December 23, 2010.

[162] Kraft, Steven P., Nuclear Energy Institute, *Used Nuclear Fuel Integrated Management*, presentation to National Association of Regulatory Utility Commissioners (NARUC), February 13, 2010.

[163] 10 C.F.R. 51.23(b).

The states of New York, Vermont, and Connecticut (later joined by New Jersey) petitioned in February 2011 to challenge NRC's rule, while NEI and Entergy intervened in support of NRC's rule.[164] NRC has indicated plans to consider the need for updating to the Waste Confidence Rule in 2019,[165] after preparing an Environmental Impact Statement.[166] Recognizing the elevated role of extended SNF storage, NRC has shifted resources for FY2012 to its "Spent Fuel Storage and Transportation Business Line" to "evaluate extended long-term storage of radioactive material," including plans for a generic environmental impact statement.[167]

In the wake of DOE's termination of the Yucca Mountain repository program, NRC is undertaking a number of efforts related to the safety of extended SNF storage. U.S. NRC Chairman Greg Jaczko stated:

> I have no doubt that we are up to the challenge of addressing the significant policy issues ahead of us. One such issue concerns our approach towards regulating interim and extended spent fuel storage. As part of our Waste Confidence decision, the Commission initiated a comprehensive review of this regulatory framework. This multi-year effort will (1) identify near-term regulatory improvements to current licensing, inspection, and enforcement programs; (2) enhance the technical and regulatory basis for extended storage and transportation; and (3) identify long-term policy changes needed to ensure safe extended storage and transportation. As the question of permanent disposal is for the Congress or the courts to decide, the Commission has been clear that it was neither assuming nor endorsing indefinite, onsite storage by ordering these actions.[168]

Among these NRC efforts is an analysis, as part of its review of the waste confidence rule and associated planning for "Extended Storage and Transportation," that will include a time frame for SNF storage until approximately 2250, which would comprise a total storage period (wet and dry) of approximately 300 years for the oldest SNF now in storage.[169]

---

[164] United States Court of Appeals for the District of Columbia Circuit, *State of New York, et al.; Petitioners, Nos. 11-1045,11-1051, -against- 11-1056, 11-1057 Nuclear Regulatory Commission, and United States of America, Respondents.*

[165] Christine Pineda, U.S. NRC, *Waste Confidence Update for Long-term Storage*, October 4, 2011. See http://pbadupws nrc.gov/docs/ML1127/ML11276A152.pdf.

[166] U.S. NRC, Catherine Haney, Director of NRC Office of Nuclear Material Safety and Safeguards, *Plan for the Long-term Update to the Waste Confidence Rule and Integration with the Extended Storage and Transportation Initiative*, SECY-11-0029, February 28, 2011.

[167] Statement By Gregory B. Jaczko, Chairman, United States Nuclear Regulatory Commission to the House Committee on Energy and Commerce, Subcommittees on Energy and Power, and Environment and the Economy, March 16, 2011.

[168] Statement by Gregory B. Jaczko, Chairman United States Nuclear Regulatory Commission to the House Committee on Energy and Commerce Subcommittees on Energy and Power, and Environment and the Economy, May 4, 2011.

[169] U.S. NRC, *Draft Report for Comment: Background and Preliminary Assumptions For an Environmental Impact Statement—Long-Term Waste Confidence Update*, December 2011, pp. 6-8 and 14; U.S. NRC, Policy Issue Information Memorandum for the Commissioners from Catherine Haney, *Plan for the Long-Term Update to the Waste Confidence Rule and Integration with the Extended Storage and Transportation Initiative*, SECY-11-0029, February 28, 2011; U.S. NRC Memorandum to Commissioners from R. W. Borchardt, *Project Plan for the Regulatory Program Review to Support Extended Storage and Transportation of Spent Nuclear Fuel*, COMSECY-10-0007, June 15, 2010; subsequently approved by U.S. NRC Memorandum to R. W. Borchardt from Annette L. Vietti-Cook, Subject: Staff Requirements, *Project Plan for Regulatory Program Review to Support Extended Storage and Transportation of Spent Nuclear Fuel*, COMSECY-10-0007, December 6, 2010.

# Options for Storing Spent Nuclear Fuel

The Administration's FY2012 budget request included no funding for Yucca Mountain repository operations or licensing activities. The House-passed Energy and Water Development Appropriations bill for FY2012 proposed to restore funding to the Yucca Mountain project, with $25 million for DOE and $20 million for NRC. The final FY2012 appropriations, however, did not include funding for Yucca Mountain activities.[170] The Administration's FY2013 request again includes no funding the Yucca Mountain repository, but instead proposes a variety of general repository studies and fuel cycle research. The House Appropriations Committee has again proposed to add funding for NRC and DOE for Yucca Mountain activities. The recent budget shifts at DOE and NRC will likely be analyzed and debated for years to come. Moreover, the recent incident at the Fukushima Dai-ichi reactor complex in Japan has spurred reexamination of SNF storage options. Accordingly, reviewing the possible options for SNF storage seems prudent.

Although a complete understanding of the events and their causes at the Fukushima Dai-ichi reactors and spent fuel pools remains incomplete, identification of some basic similarities and differences with U.S. spent fuel storage is possible. NRC established a task force to examine and report to the commission within 90 days on "the agency's regulatory requirements, programs, processes, and implementation in light of information from the Fukushima Dai-ichi site in Japan."[171] This Near-Term Task Force delivered its 90-day report and recommendations to the commission in July 2011,[172] which outlined 12 recommendations for consideration by the commission. They include a number of specific recommendations related to SNF storage safety, largely focused on backup power reliability and monitoring capabilities.[173] The NRC staff identified seven recommendations for near-term action, and offered this overall assessment: "To date the Task Force has not identified any issues that undermine our confidence in the continued safety and emergency planning of U.S. plants ... Task Force review is likely to recommend actions to enhance safety and preparedness."[174]

Options for SNF storage include not only *how* and *where* it is stored, but also what *management and oversight structure* is used. Each of these three issues is addressed below.

A threshold question, however, is what should be the basis for determining the scope of reasonable options for SNF storage? Identifying the reasonable options, and selecting from among them, will depend on certain assumptions and policy choices. Perhaps most importantly, the options and choices depend on the length of time until a permanent geologic repository is available. For decades, virtually every policy analysis has drawn its conclusions and recommendations based on certain assumptions about the opening date for the disposal repository.[175] If that date is delayed indefinitely, it opens many of these earlier assumptions,

---

[170] See CRS Report R41908, *Energy and Water Development: FY2012 Appropriations*, coordinated by Carl E. Behrens.

[171] U.S. NRC, "NRC Appoints Task Force Members and Approves Charter for Review of Agency's Response to Japan Nuclear Event," Press Release No. 11-062, April 1, 2011, http://pbadupws nrc.gov/docs/ML1109/ML110910479.pdf.

[172] U.S. NRC, *Safety Through Defense-in-Depth*, July 2011, p. 46. See http://pbadupws nrc.gov/docs/ML1118/ML111861807.pdf.

[173] Ibid.

[174] Lawrence Kokajko (U.S. Nuclear Regulatory Commission), *Recent NRC Actions Involving Spent Nuclear Fuel Storage*, presentation to the Blue Ribbon Commission on America's Nuclear Future, May 13, 2011.

[175] Monitored Retrievable Storage Review Commission, *Nuclear Waste: Is There a Need for Federal Interim Storage?*, (continued...)

analyses, and conclusions to reevaluation. As discussed above, uncertainty about the prospects for a permanent disposal repository highlights the need for long-term SNF storage. This report does not make any projections about the timing or path forward for the proposed repository.

Several other assumptions and variables could affect the options for SNF storage, including the amount of SNF generated as a result of reactor license renewal (or denial), the number and frequency of new reactor starts, potential impacts of climate change (sea level rise and more frequent and extreme weather events), or new technical developments; such factors are beyond the scope this report but warrant consideration in a more comprehensive analysis.

## Options for *How* to Store SNF

To consider *how* SNF is stored, there are essentially two options available: wet storage pools and dry cask. Few debate that dry cask storage provides greater safety than wet storage pools. The questions on which there are diverse views include (1) whether wet storage pools provide "adequate" safety, (2) whether the added safety of dry casks is worth the added short-term costs and the potential safety risks during the transfer process, and (3) whether either technology provides adequate safety under extended storage periods (more than 100 years) and under previously unforeseen occurrences.

To some extent, a simple comparison of the two SNF technologies is not appropriate because they are intended to perform somewhat different functions. Wet storage pools provide certain capabilities that dry casks cannot, such as radiological shielding and cooling necessary for intensely radioactive SNF immediately after discharge from reactors. Dry casks, on the other hand, provide adequate shielding and cooling for SNF that has been discharged from reactors at least one to five years. In addition, dry cask storage includes SNF preparation that is a step toward transportation to a repository or a consolidated storage facility (e.g., drying, inert gas, and enclosure in a cask that is typically designed to be transportable) that provides a link in the steps toward final permanent geologic repository disposal.

Notwithstanding this widespread confidence in dry cask storage, this linkage from storage to disposal, however, remains potentially incomplete. One of the significant challenges to managing SNF storage using dry casks is the lingering uncertainty about the approval for the transportation canister. Most of the SNF currently stored in dry casks is contained within an inner multipurpose container that is expected to be used to ship the SNF to a repository and be an essential barrier to prevent release of the radioactive waste after disposal. Prior to the termination of the Yucca Mountain repository program, DOE was funding the development of "Transportation, Aging and Disposal" (TAD) SNF canisters. The goal of the TAD program was to allow spent fuel assemblies discharged from nuclear reactors to be placed into sealed canisters at the reactor sites and remain in the same sealed canisters through ultimate disposal in a deep geologic repository.[176] In addition, NRC has indicated that potential new fuels, such as fuels having different cladding, internal materials, different assembly designs, and different operating conditions, and fuels with

---

(...continued)

*Report of the Monitored Retrievable Storage Review Commission*, November 1, 1989.

[176] U.S. DOE, Office of Civilian Radioactive Waste Management, *Civilian Radioactive Waste Systems: Transportation, Aging and Disposal System Performance Specifications*, Rev. 1, DOE/RW-0585, March 2008.

higher burn-up than current limits may need further review to demonstrate that extended storage can be accomplished safely.[177]

As described above, some have expressed concern about the safety of wet pool storage of SNF. Utilities have continued to use wet pool storage largely because it is viewed as adequately safe, it is legally permitted, and shifting to dry cask storage for sufficiently cooled SNF would incur costs many would view as therefore unnecessary. Nuclear power plant operators must generally justify costs to stockholders and public utility commissions, as well as compete for grid dispatch based partly on costs. Accordingly, they seek to maximize the utilization of existing capacity for storage of SNF in wet storage pools before spending money on new, dry cask storage. Hence, the practice has generally been for utilities to move SNF to dry casks only when necessary after space in existing wet pools has been exhausted using approved dense packing procedures.[178] To do otherwise could be viewed by some as spending money unnecessarily before it is warranted or required.

Two comparisons are possible in determining whether shifting to dry cask storage as soon as possible is warranted: (a) Does the current storage system "provide reasonable assurance of adequate protection?," and (b) Does dry cask storage provide sufficiently greater safety compared to wet storage pools to justify the cost and potential risks of transferring the SNF (i.e., comparing "wet to dry")?

Some have argued that the potential risks from dense packing of SNF in wet pools justify a requirement to shift SNF to dry casks as soon as it has cooled.[179] Those arguments contend not merely that dry casks provide *better* protection, but that SNF storage pools fail to provide *adequate* protection, especially given the relatively large inventory of radioactive materials being stored in many SNF pools, compared to operating reactor cores. This concern was elevated after the disaster at the Fukushima Dai-ichi reactors that highlighted specific concerns about the potential for simultaneous failure sequences. Wet storage relies on active pumping and filtration systems that require electric power for operation. NRC regards SNF storage as generally posing little risk if effective precautions are taken. NRC's website describing the two SNF storage options concludes, "[t]he NRC believes spent fuel pools and dry casks both provide adequate protection of the public health and safety and the environment. Therefore there is no pressing safety or security reason to mandate earlier transfer of fuel from pool to cask."[180] Hence,

---

[177] U.S. Nuclear Regulatory Commission, "Consideration of Environmental Impacts of Temporary Storage of Spent Fuel After Cessation of Reactor Operations; Waste Confidence Decision Update; Final Rule," 75 *Federal Register* 81032, December 23, 2010.

[178] "Dense packing" allows plant operators to store more SNF in a given amount of wet storage pool space by replacing the storage racks. Also, the capacity of an SNF storage pool is generally defined as "full" when there is sufficient remaining capacity to hold one full core load for normal refueling operations and to provide space in case more storage capacity is needed in the event of an accident.

[179] Zhang, Hui (Harvard Belfer Center on Controlling the Atom), *Radiological Terrorism: Sabotage of Spent Fuel Pools*. INESAP: International Network of Engineers and Scientists Against Proliferation no. 22 (December 2003): 75-78. Wald, Matthew, *New York Times*, "Danger of Spent Fuel Outweighs Reactor Threat," March 17, 2011; Frank N. Von Hippel, "It Could Happen Here" (Op-Ed), *New York Times*, March 23, 2011; and Robert Alvarez, *Spent Nuclear Fuel Pools in the U.S.: Reducing the Deadly Risks of Storage*, Institute for Policy Studies, May 2011.

[180] Nuclear Regulatory Commission, *Spent Fuel Storage in Pools and Dry Casks—Key Points and Questions & Answers*, 2011, http://www.nrc.gov/waste/spent-fuel-storage/faqs html. Another NRC website similarly concludes, "There are two acceptable storage methods for spent fuel after it is removed from the reactor core...." See http://www nrc.gov/waste/spent- fuel-storage html.

---

compared to its mandate to provide "adequate protection," NRC has concluded that both technologies meet that goal.

Some have made a separate argument that dry casks provide safer SNF storage than wet pools. In its post-9/11 assessment of the safety and security of SNF storage, the National Academy of Sciences/National Research Council (NAS) Committee on the Safety and Security of Commercial Spent Nuclear Fuel Storage "judges that dry cask storage has several potential safety and security advantages over pool storage."[181] In the report's recommendation that has been cited frequently and interpreted diversely, NAS urged, "Depending on the outcome of plant-specific vulnerability analyses described in the committee's classified report, the [NRC] might determine that earlier movements of spent fuel from pools into cask storage would be prudent to reduce the potential consequences of terrorist attacks on pools at some commercial nuclear plants."

NRC's response to the NAS report focused on the question of whether wet pools and dry casks were *adequate*, rather than whether dry casks were *preferable*:

> [S]torage of spent fuel in both [wet storage pools] and in dry storage casks provides reasonable assurance that public health and safety, the environment, and the common defense and security will be adequately protected. The NRC will continue to evaluate the results of the ongoing plant-specific assessments and, based upon new information, would evaluate whether any change to its spent fuel storage policy is warranted.[182]

> The NRC believes spent fuel pools and dry casks both provide adequate protection of the public health and safety and the environment. Therefore there is no pressing safety or security reason to mandate earlier transfer of fuel from pool to cask.[183]

NRC has generally limited its statements on SNF storage options to whether they provide reasonable assurance of adequate protection, rather than comparing one technology with another. NRC Chairman Greg Jaczko was quoted, however, in a recent newspaper interview: "It's like the difference between buying one ticket in the Powerball lottery and 10 tickets."[184] Another NRC official went further, comparing the equivalency of dry cask storage to wet pool storage, saying, "I think you have equal risk in both," and that federal policies consider both "equally safe, but they rely on different things to achieve that safety."[185]

The Nuclear Waste Technical Review Board concluded in 2010 that "the experience gained to date in the dry storage of spent fuel, demonstrates that used fuel can be safely stored in the short term and then transported for additional storage, processing, or repository disposal without concern."[186]

---

[181] National Academy of Sciences, National Research Council, Committee on the Safety and Security of Commercial Spent Nuclear Fuel Storage, *Safety and Security of Commercial Spent Nuclear fuel Storage: Public Report*, 2006, p. 68.

[182] Letter from Nils Diaz, Chairman of U.S. NRC to Senator Pete Domenici; with accompanying report: *U.S. Nuclear Regulatory Commission, Report to Congress on the National Academy of Sciences Study on the Safety and Security of Commercial Spent Nuclear Fuel Storage*, March 14, 2005.

[183] NRC web page: *Spent Fuel Storage in Pools and Dry Casks—Key Points and Questions & Answers*, http://www.nrc.gov/waste/spent-fuel-storage/faqs.html.

[184] Wald, Matthew L., "A Safer Nuclear Crypt," *New York Times*, July 5, 2011.

[185] Jeff Montgomery, "Delaware Energy: PSEG may make small changes for safety," *Delaware News Journal*, May 18, 2011.

[186] United States Nuclear Waste Technical Review Board, *Evaluation of the Technical Basis for Extended Dry Storage* (continued...)

---

The merits of wet pool storage versus dry casks continue to be debated, with some arguing that the risks of continued storage in wet pools, at high-density configurations, requiring reliable power for cooling water, is too high a risk, while others argue that risks are relatively low, and the increased risk during the operation to move the SNF from the pools to dry casks exceeds the value of incremental safety improvement, and that the probabilities of a mishap with either technology are low and virtually indistinguishable.

Many have observed that the dry casks at the Fukushima Dai-ichi plant were unharmed despite the earthquake and subsequent tsunami, whereas the wet SNF storage pools that were located within the same containment structure as the reactors were damaged but not the wet storage pool outside the reactor building. The damage to the wet storage pools inside the reactor buildings occurred largely as a result of the hydrogen explosions and resulting structural collapse into the pools, exacerbated by the loss of power and subsequent lack of operating monitoring instrumentation in the pools.[187] Despite this extraordinary damage, the SNF in the pools appears to have been largely unharmed. Some nuclear critics argue that the magnitude of the radioactive material inventory in wet storage pools warrants protection from the risks of a possible release from any of a number of scenarios, including station blackout or an airplane strike.[188]

Some have argued that SNF should be transferred to dry storage after the necessary cooling-off period in wet pool storage. NRC has examined this issue and determined that transfer of SNF to dry storage is not necessary to provide reasonable assurance of adequate safety. Examining the technical merits for such a requirement is beyond the scope of this report. Most recently, NRC staff, in its Near-Term Task Force recommendations from the Fukushima Dai-ichi accident, did not recommend a requirement to transfer SNF from wet to dry storage.[189] NRC has issued orders requiring additional monitoring of SNF storage and safeguards against station blackout and loss-of-power situations, which could add to the cost of maintaining wet pool storage.[190] These added costs, combined with the uncertainty about a permanent geologic repository, could increase the already accelerating rate of transfer from wet pools to dry storage. A shift of all SNF older than five years from wet pools to dry storage would more than triple the amount of SNF in dry cask storage.[191] If this shift were to occur, it would result in 85% of the total SNF stored in dry casks

---

(...continued)

*and Transportation of Used Nuclear Fuel*, December 2010, http://www.nwtrb.gov/reports/eds-final.pdf.

[187] Yoichi Funabashi and Kay Kitazawa, "Fukushima in Review: A Complex Disaster, a Disastrous Response," *Bulletin of the Atomic Scientists*, March 1, 2012 (this article summarizes a more detailed report published simultaneously in Japanese, by the Rebuild Japan Initiative Foundation); and Institute for Nuclear Power Operations, *Special Report on the Nuclear Accident at the Fukushima Daiichi Nuclear Power Station*, INPO 11-005, Rev. 0, November 2011.

[188] Robert Alvarez, *Spent Nuclear Fuel Pools in the U.S.: Reducing the Deadly Risks of Storage*, Institute for Policy Studies, May 2011.

[189] R. W. Borchardt, Executive Director for Operations, U.S. NRC, Policy Issue Memorandum for the Commissioners, "Recommended Actions to be Taken Without Delay from the Near-Term Task Force Report," SECY-11-124, September 9, 2011. The staff recommendations were largely accepted by the commission: see Annette L. Vietti-Cook, Memorandum to R. W. Borchardt, "Staff Recommendations—SECY-11-0124, "Recommended Actions to be Taken Without Delay From the Near-term Task Force Report," October 11, 2011.

[190] U.S. NRC, "Issuance of Order to Modify Licenses with Regard to Reliable Spent Fuel Pool Instrumentation," EA-12051, March 12, 2012.

[191] Currently, the inventory of SNF in dry casks is 18,112 MTU. The inventory of SNF, in both wet and dry storage, older than five years is approximately 57,450 MTU (assuming 2,000 MTU fresh SNF generated per year and a total inventory of 67,450 MTU). If any SNF in wet storage currently older than 5 years were transferred to dry storage (approximately 39,338 MTU), it would require a shift of about 80% of the current SNF inventory in wet pools. Although these estimates provide a general idea of the quantities involved, these exact amounts would not likely occur (continued...)

---

(instead of the current 25% of SNF in dry casks). To accommodate this number of transfers from wet storage pools, more than 2,700 new dry casks would be required.[192]

NRC currently provides specific technical requirements for both wet and dry cask storage, and points to this system as a reason there is no pressing safety or security reason to mandate earlier transfer of fuel from pool to cask (see "Hazards and Potential Risks Associated with SNF Storage" above).[193]

Because of the increasing use of dry cask storage, NRC's and industry's systems for implementing these requirements may require modification for a larger number of sites. A recent review by the NRC Office of Inspector General (OIG) evaluated NRC's process for inspecting the safety and security of dry cask storage. The OIG review did not identify any current technical risks with SNF storage using dry casks, but noted that NRC lacks an adequately centralized, consistent system for conducting dry cask inspection, including staffing and training. It found that NRC needed to address this issue because dry cask storage was the most likely method for additional storage capacity, and that all reactors are expected to require dry cask storage by 2025. As dry cask increasingly becomes the predominant method for SNF storage, rather than a supplement to wet pool storage, NRC would need to step up the level of staffing, training, and procedural discipline to ensure effective and consistent inspections.[194] The OIG findings did not identify any technical failures with dry casks, but rather recommended adjustments in NRC management to make oversight and inspections more systematic. NRC has begun implementing these improvements in the dry cask inspection program.[195]

NRC's recent *Near-Term Task Force Review of Insights from the Fukushima Dai-ichi Accident* did not include a mandate to switch from wet to dry storage among its recommendations for considerations by the commission. The Near-Term Task Force recommended, instead, "enhancing spent fuel pool makeup capability and instrumentation for the spent fuel pool" (Section 4.2.4) and a number of actions to address site blackout mitigation and preparedness.[196] The commission staff review of the task force recommendations subsequently found there was "no imminent risk from continued operation and licensing activities" and recommended action on several task force recommendations, including addressing site blackout issues (e.g., establish a "coping time of 72

---

(...continued)

because by the time all of the current SNF storage were shifted to dry cask, there would be more aged fuel in storage and more fresh fuel generated.

[192] This estimate of 2,732 new dry casks assumes 50 assemblies per dry cask, based on the 2009 history of 5,567 assemblies loaded into 130 dry casks (43 assemblies per cask), and the 2010 history of 8,606 assemblies transferred to 140 casks (61 assemblies per cask) and 80% of the 170,734 assemblies in wet storage as of the end of 2010. It also assumes, unrealistically, instant transfer, which would actually require several years to accomplish, which could potentially allow for reuse of transport casks. Again, the exact number would depend on the time period over which the shift would occur.

[193] U.S. NRC, "NRC Standard Review Plan for Dry Cask Storage Systems" (NUREG-1536).193 Nuclear Regulatory Commission, "Spent Fuel Storage in Pools and Dry Casks Key Points and Questions & Answers," 2011, http://www.nrc.gov/waste/spent-fuel-storage/faqs.html.

[194] NRC Office of Inspector General, "Audit Report: Audit of NRC's Oversight of Independent Spent Fuel Storage Installations Safety," OIG-11-A-12, May 19, 2011.

[195] U.S. NRC, Memorandum from Stephen D. Dingbaum to R. William Borchardt, *Status Of Recommendations: Audit Of NRC's Oversight Of Independent Spent Fuel Storage Installations Safety* (OIG-11-A-12), June 30, 2011.

[196] U.S. NRC, *Recommendations for Enhancing Reactors Safety in the 21ˢᵗ Century: The Near-Term Task Force Review of Insights from the Fukushima Dai-ichi Accident*, July 12, 2011, http://pbadupws nrc.gov/docs/ML1118/ML111861807.pdf.

hours for core and spent fuel pool cooling ..." under 10 C.F.R. 50.54(hh)(2)). The staff review recommended deferring action, however, on other task force recommendations related to SNF management, based on the need for additional review, in part to consider related regulatory actions, such as seismic qualification and instrumentation requirements.[197]

## Options for *Where* to Store SNF

The options for *where* to store SNF include alternatives ranging from continued decentralized storage at dozens of locations to some combination of consolidated or centralized storage facilities. Among the reasons for considering alternative storage locations are the costs incurred by multiple reactor locations, and concern that nuclear power plants were not originally located and designed to serve as indefinite SNF storage sites. In addition, some analysts have recommended long-term interim storage to improve safety and reduce pressure on establishing a repository in a forced technical and political environment.[198] The SNF storage option most often debated, and most recently recommended by the Blue Ribbon Commission (BRC), is the establishment of centralized storage locations, or consolidated storage, for stranded SNF.

Any evaluation of options for where to store SNF begins with the current situation, which includes the location of existing SNF (see above section) and the statute governing SNF management, the Nuclear Waste Policy Act (NWPA). The current U.S. inventory of SNF is more than 67,000 MTU, and growing by approximately 2,000 MTU per year. Various studies have projected future inventories of SNF requiring storage and disposal. The results depend on assumptions about the rate at which SNF is generated, which depends on assumptions about reactor operations, license renewals, and new reactor construction. For example, a 1995 DOE study projected that SNF storage would reach approximately 86,000 MTU in about 2030 and level off unless a significant number of new reactors are ordered, constructed, and operated.[199] Future inventory levels, which depend on capacity factors at, and number of reactors in operation, and discharge rates for SNF, could have an impact on the need for storage and disposal capacity.

Secretary of Energy Spencer Abraham cited security concerns in the wake of the September 11, 2001, attacks as a basis for relocating high-level waste from at-reactor storage to Nevada surface storage.[200] Others have noted that at least some of the spent fuel and high-level waste will remain at the same temporary storage locations for as long as the facilities operate. Storage of discharged spent fuel will require at-reactor storage for at least one to five years to allow the SNF to cool sufficiently to allow transfer to a dry cask for storage or transport.

---

[197] R. W. Borchardt, Executive Director for Operations, U.S. NRC, Policy Issue Memorandum for the Commissioners, "Recommended Actions to be Taken Without Delay from the Near-Term Task Force Report," SECY-11-0124, September 9, 2011; and R. William Borchardt, U.S. NRC, "Briefing on the Japan Near Term Task Force Report— Prioritization of Recommendations," October 11, 2011; and transcript of meeting at http://www.nrc.gov/reading-rm/doc-collections/commission/tr/2011/20111011.pdf.

[198] See Bunn, Matthew, et al., *Interim Storage of Spent Nuclear Fuel: A Safe, Flexible, and Cost-Effective Near Term Approach to Spent Nuclear Fuel Management*, Harvard Press, Cambridge, MA, Harvard University Project on Managing the Atom and University of Tokyo Project on Nuclear Energy, 2001, http://belfercenter ksg harvard.edu/files/spentfuel.pdf.

[199] U.S. DOE, "*Spent Fuel Storage Requirements 1994-2042*," DOE/RW-0431-Rev.1, June 1995.

[200] Letter from Spencer Abraham, Secretary of Energy, to The President, on Site Recommendation (February 14, 2002); U.S. DOE, Recommendation Of The Secretary Of Energy Regarding The Suitability Of The Yucca Mountain Site For A Repository Under The Nuclear Waste Policy Act of 1982 (February 2002), http://www.energy.gov/media/Secretary_s_Recommendation_Report.pdf.

---

The BRC draft report noted that the NWPA allows for the construction of one consolidated interim storage facility with limited capacity, and only after a nuclear waste repository is licensed.[201] This statutory limitation reflects the perennial concern that establishment of a "temporary" or interim storage site could become a de facto permanent waste repository, and could reduce the perceived need for a permanent geological repository. BRC concluded that "[o]ne or more consolidated storage facilities will be required, independent of the schedule for opening a repository."[202] BRC explicitly recommended that the NWPA be "modified to allow for multiple storage facilities with adequate capacity to be sited, licensed and constructed when needed."[203] BRC's Transportation and Storage Subcommittee had earlier signaled its support for consolidated interim storage in its draft May 2011 report, which indicated that a central interim storage location could provide significant benefits, including reduced costs, improved safety, and increased overall confidence in nuclear power as a viable long-term energy source.[204]

The BRC recommendation is consistent with a major report earlier in the year by the Massachusetts Institute of Technology (MIT), which stated, "[t]he possibility of storage for a century, which is longer than the anticipated lifetimes of nuclear reactors, suggests that the U.S. should move toward centralized storage sites—starting with SNF from decommissioned reactor sites and in support of a long-term SNF management strategy."[205] Similarly, in testimony before BRC, a longtime nuclear analyst from Harvard University urged BRC to follow the advice of the bipartisan National Commission on Energy Policy, which recommended that Congress "[a]mend the Nuclear Waste Policy Act to make clear that interim storage and federal responsibility for waste disposal are sufficient to satisfy the Nuclear Regulatory Commission's waste [confidence] rule."[206] Except for state requirements, this need to address long-term SNF storage is not a near-term limitation on building new nuclear power plants.

Senators Lisa Murkowski and Mary Landrieu proposed legislation in June 2011 (S. 1320, the Nuclear Fuel Storage Improvement Act) intended to help establish up to two interim nuclear waste storage sites. The bill includes provisions to support DOE in paying local governments who offer to host interim spent fuel storage facilities using the Nuclear Waste Fund for these payments. It also directs DOE to arrange for the transportation of the SNF to the interim site.

The idea of consolidated interim storage has been debated for many years. The concerns about consolidated interim storage expressed by some include (1) potentially reducing pressure on decision makers to agree on a permanent repository because the problem will appear to have been "solved" and because of a resulting concern that storage sites would become de facto repositories; (2) protracted delays because of the difficulty in finding a willing host community for SNF storage, which could divert resources from other useful efforts (e.g., safety and security of

---

[201] 42 U.S.C. 10168(d).

[202] Blue Ribbon Commission on America's Nuclear Future, *Report to the Secretary of Energy*, January 2012, http://brc.gov/sites/default/files/documents/brc_finalreport_jan2012.pdf.

[203] Ibid.

[204] Transportation and Storage Subcommittee; Report to the Full Commission; Updated Report, Blue Ribbon Commission on America's Nuclear Future, January 2012. See http://www.brc.gov/sites/default/files/documents/final_updated_ts_report_012612.pdfhttp://brc.gov/sites/default/files/documents/draft_ts_report_6-1-11.pdf.

[205] Massachusetts Institute of Technology, *The Future of the Nuclear Fuel Cycle: An Interdisciplinary MIT Study*, MIT, Cambridge, MA, 2011. The MIT study also recommended that "planning for the long term interim storage of spent nuclear fuel—for about a century—should be part of fuel cycle design." Ibid. at page xi.

[206] Bunn, Matthew (Harvard University), testimony before the Blue Ribbon Commission on America's Nuclear Future, May 25, 2010.

---

existing SNF storage and repository siting); and (3) potentially higher net risks if the SNF were to require multiple moves to transport it to the interim site and again to the repository (depending on risk reduction from moving SNF from existing storage locations).

Many have found common ground on the need to consolidate storage of SNF that is located where a reactor or other nuclear facilities have been shut down (i.e., "stranded" SNF sites). If the SNF at these locations were consolidated to a new or existing storage site, it would have the effect of reducing the number of storage sites and reducing many fixed overhead costs (e.g., security and maintenance). It could also add a new storage site or sites to the map, depending on whether an existing storage site was used. There will be a temporary need for wet storage even after reactors at a site have ceased operation to allow time for the SNF to cool sufficiently (one to five years) to be transferred to dry cask storage.

Consolidating current inventories of SNF reduces, but cannot eliminate, the need for spent fuel at these sites. At sites where the reactor continues to operate, SNF will continue to be stored, at a minimum, to allow for cooling of newly generated SNF before it can be moved. Moving SNF from the 10 commercial "stranded" SNF sites[207] to a consolidation site would have the effect of reducing the number of sites requiring security and safeguards, thereby potentially reducing storage costs, or allowing more resources to be devoted to safety and security at the consolidated site, compared to multiple sites. There may be some incremental additional risk in transporting the SNF to a consolidated site. The risks and costs of continuing to store the SNF at the reactor site would have to be compared to the risks of transferring to another location. The United States has some significant experience with safely transporting SNF, largely through the DOE Foreign Research Reactor SNF return program and limited intra-utility transfers. In this program, DOE has, with no significant safety incidents, returned spent fuel from countries where the United States had previously shipped nuclear materials—often weapons-grade uranium—with the expectations that the material would be shipped back to the United States after being discharged from the reactor.

## Options for SNF Management and Regulatory Oversight

To consider *alternative management and regulatory oversight structures*, there is a range of possible options, including both government and quasi-governmental entities with varying authorities and resources. For decades, Congress has charged three federal agencies with the primary responsibilities[208] for high-level nuclear waste management, including SNF: DOE has been responsible for technical evaluations of the Yucca Mountain site, preparing license application documents and eventually operating the geologic repository; the Environmental Protection Agency has been responsible for developing standards; and NRC has been responsible for the licensing process, including the geologic repository and SNF storage in wet pools and dry casks. With the termination of the Yucca Mountain repository program at DOE, civilian SNF

---

[207] This number includes all four DOE sites. The DOE reactors generally shut down in the 1980s, except for a brief restart of the K reactor at the Savannah River Site in 1991.

[208] In addition to these primary agencies responsible for the licensing of the repository, the Department of Transportation is charged with ensuring that waste carriers comply with routing regulations and guidelines, and the Mine Safety and Health Administration of the Department of Labor is responsible for ensuring the health and safety of underground workers at the Yucca Mountain facility.

analysis has been transferred from DOE's former Office of Civilian Radioactive Waste Management to DOE's Office of Nuclear Energy.[209]

Various institutional structures and models have been proposed to manage nuclear waste in place of the current responsibility given to DOE, mandated by the NWPA. For example, Senator George Voinovich repeatedly introduced the U. S. Nuclear Fuel Management Corporation Establishment Act,[210] which would establish a government corporation with a bipartisan board of directors appointed by the President and confirmed by the Senate.

The Blue Ribbon Commission (BRC) concluded that "a new, single-purpose organization is needed to develop and implement a focused, integrated program for the transportation, storage, and disposal of nuclear waste in the United States," and that "moving responsibility ... outside DOE ... offers the best chance for future success."[211] Again, a similar recommendation had been included in the MIT report, which recommended "that a new quasi-government waste management organization be established to implement the nation's waste management program."[212] The BRC recommendation to change the institutional structure for managing SNF by creating a new federal corporation "dedicated solely to implementing the waste management program and empowered with the authority and resources to succeed"[213] was considered by some to be the "centerpiece of the BRC's recommendations,"[214] though they criticized it as falling short of their goal of a market-based private SNF management system.

Some have recommended the use of existing DOE nuclear weapons facilities for storage of SNF, coupled with spending on research for new reprocessing technologies.[215] The idea of establishing a consolidated storage facility for commercial SNF at a DOE facility is part of the larger debate about whether, how, and where to establish consolidated SNF storage sites. Proposals to use DOE sites (e.g., the Savannah River Site in South Carolina) for this purpose are often linked with using existing DOE facilities, including reprocessing "canyon" buildings. Although it is beyond the scope of this report, as Congress considers the BRC recommendations for alternative nuclear waste management structures, it may useful to consider prior federal government experience in operating and providing both support and regulatory oversight for disposal repository and reprocessing efforts.

---

[209] For more details about the FY2012 budget for DOE, see CRS Report R41908, *Energy and Water Development: FY2012 Appropriations*, coordinated by Carl E. Behrens.

[210] United States Nuclear Fuel Management Corporation Establishment Act of [2008/2010], S. 3661 in the 110th Congress and S. 3322 in the 111th Congress.

[211] Blue Ribbon Commission on America's Nuclear Future, *Draft Report to the Secretary of Energy*, January 2012, p. 60.

[212] Massachusetts Institute of Technology, *The Future of the Nuclear Fuel Cycle: An Interdisciplinary MIT Study*, MIT, Cambridge, MA, 2011.

[213] Blue Ribbon Commission on America's Nuclear Future, *Draft Report to the Secretary of Energy*, January 2012, p. vii.

[214] Jack Spencer, Heritage Foundation, testimony before the Committee on Science, Space, and Technology's Energy and Environment and Investigations and Oversight Subcommittees, "Review of the Blue Ribbon Commission on America's Nuclear Future Draft Recommendations," October 27, 2011. The comments referred to are essentially identical recommendations of the BRC from its July 2011 draft report.

[215] Douglas Wyatt, Ernie Chaput, and Dean Hoffman, "Siting GNEP at the Savannah River Site: Using Legacy and Infrastructure in a Commercial Energy Park Concept," *Waste Management 2008 Conference*, 2008, Phoenix, AZ; and Central Savannah River Area Community Team, 2007, *Global Nuclear Energy Partnership Siting Study, Final Report, Energy Park on the Savannah River*, DE-FG07-06ID14794, April 30, 2007.

Managing SNF storage and disposal through reprocessing, or chemical separations, is a perennial issue, distinct from the question of storage location, that has been promoted as an SNF solution for many years.[216] Others have argued that reprocessing has already been demonstrated to be not cost-effective, to produce significant environmental problems, and potentially to affect U.S. nuclear weapons nonproliferation policy. A variety of studies have concluded that reprocessing of SNF cannot be justified on the basis of waste management advantages or economics, but many support additional investment in research and development of more cost-effective reprocessing technologies.[217] A recent MIT study concluded, for example, "[f]or the next several decades, light water reactors using the once-through fuel cycle are the preferred option for the U.S."[218] These studies generally assume other options for spent fuel management, stockpiles and prices for uranium, and the readiness of the "fast" reactors that are viewed as a method to consume plutonium generated from reprocessing. Even the strongest advocates for reprocessing do not promote near-term deployment, and instead urge more government-funded research to pursue new reprocessing technologies, concluding "there is no benefit to reprocessing at this time."[219] BRC concluded that "no currently available or reasonably foreseeable reactor and fuel cycle technology developments—including advances in reprocessing and recycling technologies—have the potential to fundamentally alter the waste management challenge this nation confronts over at least the next several decades, if not longer."[220] Many analysts have raised concerns about the proliferation policy impacts associated with reprocessing, which gave rise to the U.S. halt in reprocessing by President Gerald Ford in the 1970s. Although this presidential ban was subsequently reversed, there are currently no plans for resumption of commercial reprocessing, largely because it has not been viewed as commercially viable.[221]

---

[216] See recently William H. Miller, "Used Nuclear Fuel is Good Source of Energy; Reprocessing has Potential for U.S.," *Columbia Tribune*, December 13, 2011; Clinton Bastin, "We Need to Reprocess Spent Nuclear Fuel, and Can Do it Safely, at Reasonable Cost," 21st Century Science and Technology, Summer 2008; and William Tucker, "There Is No Such Thing as Nuclear Waste," *Wall Street Journal*, March 13, 2009.

[217] National Academy of Sciences/National Research Council, Board on Radioactive Waste Management, Nuclear Wastes: Technologies for Separations and Transmutation, National Academies Press, Washington, DC, 1996; National Academies/National Research Council, "Committee on Review of DOE's Nuclear Energy Research and Development Program," National Academies Press, Washington, DC, 2008; Frank N. von Hippel, "Nuclear Fuel Recycling: More Trouble Than It's Worth," *Scientific American*, April 28, 2008; Nuclear Energy Institute, Nuclear Waste Disposal for the Future: The Potential of Reprocessing and Recycling, 2006; Bunn, Matthew, Steve Fetter, John P. Holdren, and Bob van der Zwaan, "The Economics of Reprocessing vs. Direct Disposal of Spent Nuclear Fuel," DOE grant # DE-FG26-99FT4028 (Cambridge, MA: Project on Managing the Atom, Harvard University, 2003), December 2003; von Hippel, Frank (Princeton University), "International Impact of U.S. Spent-fuel Policy," prepared statement to the Blue Ribbon Commission on America's Nuclear Future, September 21, 2010, and Nuclear Energy Institute, *Policy Brief: Advanced Fuel-Cycle Technologies Hold Promise for Used Fuel Management Program*, March 2010, http://www.nei.org/resourcesandstats/documentlibrary/nuclearwastedisposal/policybrief/advancedfuelcycle/?page=2; Steve Fetter and Frank N. von Hippel, "Is Reprocessing Worth the Risk?" *Arms Control Today*, September 2005; Lisbeth Gronlund, David Lochbaum, and Edwin Lyman, *Nuclear power in a warming world; Assessing the Risks, Addressing the Challenges*, Union of Concerned Scientists, December 2007; Johns Hopkins University, Paul H. Nitze School of Advanced International Studies, Energy, Resources, and Environment Program, *Nuclear Fuel Cycle Report*, February 2011; and *Advanced Nuclear Fuel Cycles—Main Challenges and Strategic Choices*, EPRI, Palo Alto, CA: 2010. 1020307.

[218] Massachusetts Institute of Technology, *The Future of the Nuclear Fuel Cycle: An Interdisciplinary MIT Study*, MIT, Cambridge, MA, 2011, p. xi.

[219] Nuclear Energy Institute, *Nuclear Waste Disposal for the Future: The Potential of Reprocessing and Recycling*, 2006; and Boston Consulting Group, *Economic Assessment of Used Nuclear Fuel Management in the United States (Prepared by the Boston Consulting Group for Areva)*, July 2006.

[220] Blue Ribbon Commission on America's Nuclear Future, *Report to the Secretary of Energy*, January 2012, p. 100.

[221] U.S. Congressional Budget Office, Peter R. Orszag, "Costs of Reprocessing Versus Directly Disposing of Spent (continued...)

---

The conclusion that SNF reprocessing is not currently viable as a cost-effective alternative to storage and disposal does not necessarily mean that some viable SNF processing technology could not be developed in the future. Proponents of research on new SNF processing technologies assert that new SNF technologies would not necessarily generate the same wastes as in traditional aqueous "PUREX" reprocessing technologies, or pose a proliferation risk from separation of weapons-usable fissile materials. The Obama Administration has adopted and funded a policy consistent with the view of the chairman of the Senate Subcommittee on Clean Air and Nuclear Safety of the Environmental and Public Works Committee (Senator Thomas Carper), and the conclusions of an earlier MIT report that recommended research into new SNF processing technologies, and more fundamentally, a broader life-cycle effort to integrate fuel designs and reactors with long-term SNF disposition plans.

BRC recommended "increased federal funding be provided to the NRC to support ... ongoing work by the NRC to develop a robust ... regulatory framework for advanced nuclear energy systems ... including NRC's ongoing review of the current waste classification system. Such a framework can help guide the design of new systems and lower barriers to commercial investment by increasing confidence that new systems can be successfully licensed."[222] The nuclear industry has indicated that NRC rulemaking is needed because "the cost of the technology cannot be determined until the regulatory framework is known."[223] NRC has initiated a rulemaking to establish a licensing process for SNF reprocessing. Some nuclear critics have questioned the need for rulemaking given the lack of proposals for reprocessing.[224]

# Issues for Congress

In the United States, SNF is largely stored at reactors where the SNF was generated, using dry casks as necessary when storage pool storage capacity is exhausted. Given current prospects for adequate repository capacity and existing and growing inventories of waste, long-term (60 years beyond reactor license) or extended (more than 150 years) SNF storage is likely. While some have expressed concern about the safety of wet pool storage and preference for dry cask systems, others, including NRC, believe that sufficient regulatory controls and economic incentives exist for ensuring safe storage of SNF. Regardless of actual or perceived risk, most growth in SNF storage has been with dry systems, and the portion of SNF storage using dry cask systems, compared to wet pools, is likely to continue to increase more rapidly. The trend is driven largely by the long-term cost advantages of dry cask systems in a storage regime that now has a longer time horizon.

The current SNF storage situation could change if Congress adopts the recommendations of the Blue Ribbon Commission on America's Nuclear Future. These recommendations address where and how SNF is stored, as well as the institutional structures responsible. Areas of significant

---

(...continued)

Nuclear Fuel," Statement before the Senate Committee on Energy and Natural Resources, November 14, 2007, http://www.cbo.gov/sites/default/files/cbofiles/ftpdocs/88xx/doc8808/11-14-nuclearfuel.pdf.

[222] Blue Ribbon Commission on America's Nuclear Future, *Report to the Secretary of Energy*, January 2012, p. xiv, http://brc.gov/sites/default/files/documents/brc_finalreport_jan2012.pdf.

[223] E-mail from Rodney McCullum, Nuclear Energy Institute, December 11, 2011.

[224] Fettus, Geoff, Tom Cochran, and Christopher Paine, NRDC Comments on Draft Regulatory Basis for Potential Rulemaking on Spent Nuclear Fuel Reprocessing Facilities, Docket ID NRC-2010-0267, July 7, 2011.

uncertainty include the likelihood of success of siting a "temporary" centralized consolidated storage site, the establishment of a new agency or federal corporation to manage SNF, and the prospects for success in developing advanced nuclear fuel cycles that address the economic, environmental, and proliferation issues that have foiled past efforts.

The Senate Energy and Water Development appropriations bill for FY2013 includes provisions to help fund efforts to adopt the BRC recommendations.[225] The Senate committee included language (S. 2465, Section 312) authorizing a pilot program to demonstrate one or more consolidated interim storage facilities for SNF and high-level waste. Any consolidated storage site would require the consent of the affected state governor, local government of jurisdiction, affected Indian tribes, and Congress. The Senate panel directed DOE to use $2 million of its program direction funding for the pilot program, along with $17.7 million in unobligated prior-year appropriations from the Nuclear Waste Fund. The bill would also require DOE, within 120 days of enactment, to submit to Congress a Pilot Program Plan and issue a Request for Proposals for Cooperative Agreements to implement the program. Among the issues to be addressed by DOE is the potential cost savings through consolidation of SNF storage. Also, the Senate Energy and Natural Resources Committee is reported to be developing legislation to address BRC recommendations.[226] The House bill does not address SNF storage but provides $25 million in FY2013 to resume Yucca Mountain disposal repository activities.

---

[225] See http://www.appropriations.senate.gov/news.cfm?method=news.view&id=eaa626fc-9ba7-4477-ae48-25767c9ae814.

[226] Hannah Northey and Nick Juliano, "Bipartisan Senators Begin Legislative Push For Waste Solution," *Environment and Energy Daily*, April 25, 2012.

# Appendix. U.S. Spent Nuclear Fuel Storage Inventories

## Table A-1. Alphabetical List of 35 States Where Spent Nuclear Fuel is Stored

As of December 31, 2011 (see **Table 1** for data sorted by mass of SNF storage)

| State (15 states have no stored SNF)[a] | Number of Facilities | Number of Sites | "Stranded" SNF Storage Sites[b] | MTU Wet Storage | MTU Dry Cask | MTU Total SNF | Assemblies Wet Storage | Assemblies Dry Cask | Assemblies Total SNF | Table Notes |
|---|---|---|---|---|---|---|---|---|---|---|
| Alabama | 5 | 2 | - | 2,647 | 540 | 3,187 | 10,978 | 2,180 | 13,158 | |
| Arizona | 3 | 1 | - | 1,052 | 903 | 1,955 | 2,490 | 2,136 | 4,626 | |
| Arkansas | 2 | 1 | - | 607 | 726 | 1,333 | 1,336 | 1,600 | 2,936 | |
| California | 7 | 4 | 2 | 2,017 | 916 | 2,933 | 4,750 | 2,486 | 7,236 | b & g |
| Colorado | 1 | 1 | 1 | 0 | 15 | 15 | - | 2,208 | 2,208 | b & f |
| Connecticut | 4 | 2 | 1 | 1,439 | 613 | 2,052 | 5,050 | 1,467 | 6,517 | b & g |
| Florida | 5 | 3 | - | 2,511 | 445 | 2,956 | 5,859 | 1,024 | 6,883 | f |
| Georgia | 4 | 2 | - | 2,018 | 592 | 2,610 | 7,366 | 3,264 | 10,630 | |
| Idaho | 1 | 1 | 1 | 50 | 81 | 131 | 144 | 177 | 321 | b |
| Illinois | 15 | 8 | 2 | 6,900 | 1,791 | 8,691 | 28,242 | 9,625 | 37,867 | b & c |
| Iowa | 1 | 1 | - | 259 | 217 | 476 | 1,452 | 1,220 | 2,672 | |
| Kansas | 1 | 1 | - | 646 | 0 | 646 | 1,434 | - | 1,434 | |
| Louisiana | 2 | 2 | - | 1,014 | 235 | 1,249 | 3,861 | 1,148 | 5,009 | |
| Maine | 1 | 1 | 1 | 0 | 542 | 542 | - | 1,438 | 1,438 | b |
| Maryland | 2 | 1 | - | 531 | 808 | 1,339 | 1,197 | 1,824 | 3,021 | f |
| Massachusetts | 2 | 2 | 1 | 542 | 122 | 664 | 3,082 | 533 | 3,615 | b |
| Michigan | 5 | 4 | 1 | 2,058 | 502 | 2,560 | 6,495 | 1,537 | 8,032 | b & f |
| Minnesota | 3 | 2 | - | 678 | 525 | 1,203 | 2,645 | 1,770 | 4,415 | g |
| Mississippi | 1 | 1 | - | 602 | 203 | 805 | 3,428 | 1,156 | 4,584 | |
| Missouri | 1 | 1 | - | 679 | 0 | 679 | 1,696 | - | 1,696 | |

| State (15 states have no stored SNF)[a] | Number of Facilities | Number of Sites | "Stranded" SNF Storage Sites[b] | MTU Wet Storage | MTU Dry Cask | MTU Total SNF | Assemblies Wet Storage | Assemblies Dry Cask | Assemblies Total SNF | Table Notes |
|---|---|---|---|---|---|---|---|---|---|---|
| Nebraska | 2 | 2 | - | 650 | 203 | 853 | 2,825 | 808 | 3,633 | g |
| New Hampshire | 1 | 1 | - | 455 | 93 | 548 | 944 | 192 | 1,136 | h |
| New Jersey | 4 | 2 | - | 2,025 | 529 | 2,554 | 7,489 | 2,535 | 10,024 | b & f |
| New York | 7 | 4 | - | 3,082 | 495 | 3,577 | 12,466 | 1,820 | 14,286 | |
| North Carolina | 5 | 3 | - | 3,018 | 544 | 3,562 | 10,612 | 1,480 | 12,092 | |
| Ohio | 2 | 2 | - | 1,083 | 34 | 1,117 | 4,542 | 72 | 4,614 | |
| Oregon | 1 | 1 | 1 | 0 | 345 | 345 | - | 801 | 801 | b |
| Pennsylvania | 9 | 5 | - | 4,606 | 1,459 | 6,065 | 20,898 | 8,424 | 29,322 | d |
| South Carolina | 8 | 5 | 1 | 2,236 | 1,808 | 4,044 | 5,001 | 3,896 | 8,897 | b & e |
| Tennessee | 3 | 2 | - | 1,095 | 470 | 1,565 | 2,386 | 1,024 | 3,410 | |
| Texas | 4 | 2 | - | 2,121 | 0 | 2,121 | 4,522 | - | 4,522 | |
| Vermont | 1 | 1 | - | 513 | 111 | 624 | 2,815 | 612 | 3,427 | |
| Virginia | 4 | 2 | - | 970 | 1,477 | 2,447 | 2,120 | 3,229 | 5,349 | f |
| Washington | 2 | 2 | 1 | 319 | 339 | 658 | 1,715 | 1,836 | 3,551 | b |
| Wisconsin | 4 | 3 | 1 | 915 | 419 | 1,334 | 2,603 | 1,088 | 3,691 | b & f |
| U.S. Total Commercial Site Storage | 119 | 74 | 10 | 46,733 | 15,859 | 62,592 | 165,583 | 56,493 | 222,076 | |
| U.S. Total DOE Site Storage | 4 | 4 | 4 | 2,605 | 2,243 | 4,848 | 6,860 | 8,117 | 14,977 | |

Source: The primary source for these data is the Nuclear Energy Institute (NEI) report, "2011 Used Fuel Data," prepared by Gutherman Technical Associates, January 14, 2012. Site-specific data on sites with no operating reactors ("Storage-only Sites") is derived largely from U.S. DOE, Report to Congress on the Demonstration of the Interim Storage of Spent Nuclear Fuel from Decommissioned Nuclear Power Reactor Sites, DOE/RW-0596, December 2008. Data for DOE sites were generally from Frank Marcinowski, Overview of DOE's Spend Nuclear Fuel & High Level Waste; Presentation to the Blue Ribbon Commission on America's Nuclear Future, U.S. DOE, March 25, 2010.

a. There are currently 15 states with no commercial SNF storage (there may be temporary and relatively small-scale storage of SNF from non-power generating research and academic reactors): Alaska, Delaware, Hawaii, Indiana, Kentucky, Montana, Nevada, New Mexico, North Dakota, Oklahoma, Rhode Island, South Dakota, Utah, West Virginia, Wyoming.

b. "Stranded" is generally used to refer to SNF stored where the nuclear reactor that generated the SNF has ceased operating and been decommissioned, and the SNF remains at the site. In some cases the wet storage pools have been dismantled and the SNF is stored in dry casks. In the case of the Morris, IL, site, the "stranded" SNF was shipped from other reactor sites for a proposed reprocessing facility that never operated., and no reactor has ever operated at the site. The number of "stranded" SNF storage sites here does not include sites where SNF is stored at decommissioned reactor sites co-located with operating reactors (e.g., San Onofre (CA), Dresden 1 (IL), or Indian Point (NY)). The table does not include DOE nuclear weapons facilities in Colorado, Idaho, South Carolina, and Washington that store commercial SNF—sites where DOE reactors largely ceased operations in the 1980s.

c. Includes the Morris, IL, site, operated by GE-Hitachi, which never hosted an operating reactor or generated any SNF. The site was built to serve as an SNF reprocessing plant for which the SNF from other sites was shipped. The facility never operated, and the SNF has remained stored at the site. Many sources categorize the Morris site with dry cask storage sites, because they are all considered "Independent Spent Fuel Storage Installations" (ISFSI), although the Morris site differs from other ISFSIs because it uses wet pool storage and is categorized accordingly here.

d. Excludes SNF and debris generated at the Three Mile Island-2 facility removed after the 1979 incident and shipped to DOE's Idaho National Engineering Laboratory (now know as the "Idaho National Laboratory").

e. Includes 29 MTU of SNF, fragments, and nuclear materials stored at the Savannah River Site (SRS) near Aiken, which has been operated by DOE for nuclear weapons material production. In addition to material generated there, the SRS is used to store SNF shipped from commercial reactors (e.g., Carolinas-Virginia Tube Reactor) and from foreign and domestic research reactors using U.S.-origin fuel.

f. Does not include SNF shipped to DOE federal facilities: 8 MTU from Florida, 1 MTU from Maryland, 12 MTU from Michigan, 16 MTU from New York, 22 MTU from Virginia, and 4 MTU from Wisconsin, as well as part of the SNF from the Fort St. Vrain site in Colorado, which was shipped to Idaho.

g. Does not include SNF shipped to the Morris, IL, facility (see (b) above) from 4 states: 100 MTU from California, 34 MTU from Connecticut, 185 MTU from Minnesota, and 191 MTU from Nebraska. Includes 132 MTU shipped from other facilities in Illinois to the Morris facility.

h. The adjacent Salem 1 and 2 and Hope Creek reactors share dry cask storage facilities and could be considered three facilities on a single contiguous site.

# Author Contact Information

James D. Werner
Section Research Manager
jwerner@crs.loc.gov, 7-3862